0844 995 1214
CRUISEDIALYSIS.CO.U.K

THE DANUBE

Martin Gostelow

D1639322

JPMGUIDES

CONTENTS

rich bird life

bucolic charms

ALONG THE DANUBE

Who can hear the name Danube without thinking of that most famous of Strauss waltzes: "On the Beautiful Blue Danube"? Beautiful it certainly is, but to be honest, it's more a brownish yellow than blue, thanks to the lime and mud stirred up from the river bed. The Danube's romance lies in the medieval castles, baroque churches and rococo palaces it passes on its way through central Europe and the Balkans, as well as the historic cities that have grown up along its banks.

International River

The great waterway begins in southwest Germany at the confluence of the Brege and the Brigach, and flows through eight other countries to the sea: Austria, Slovakia, Hungary, Croatia, Serbia, Romania, Bulgaria and Ukraine. Over a stretch of just 570 m, the Danube also flows through Moldova, making it another member of the International Danube Commission. Its 2,850 km (1,770 miles) make it Europe's second longest river, after the Volga. Barge traffic starts at the cathedral town of Ulm, larger vessels at Regensburg. Today, completion of the Main–Danube Canal extends navigation from the North Sea to the Black Sea delta, more than 3,200 km (2,000 miles).

Through Austria and Hungary

The Danube crosses from Germany into Austria at Passau, established as a frontier town by the Romans. It flows through the major port town of Linz to the Habsburgs' grand imperial city of Vienna. From Slovakia's capital, Bratislava, the river follows the Hungarian border until it makes a dramatic 90-degree turn at the Danube Bend and heads south to the Hungarian capital of Budapest. Here, it cleaves through the city, separating the old hill town of Buda from the more modern and much flatter Pest. Beyond the suburbs, the river returns to its bucolic mood, flowing through flat and fertile countryside. In all, the Danube's passage through Hungary stretches for 417 km (260 miles).

Borderline

From Budapest to the Black Sea, the river has regularly acted as a border, often separating rival kingdoms—or bitter enemies. Roman sentries and Dacian warriors kept watch on each other across the lower Danube; centuries later the armies of the Habsburgs faced the Ottoman Turks. Many of the towns were founded in Roman times, and medieval fortresses, castle ruins and memorials still attest to the battles which were fought here. Under the Austro-Hungarian Monarchy (1683–1918), the countries on the middle and lower reaches seemed to be united—the first and only time that a "Confederation of the Danube" has been a reality.

Tributaries

On its way to the Black Sea, the river passes through a succession of incredibly varied landscapes. In the Great Hungarian Plain (Nagy Alföld) it is joined by major tributaries: the Drava, the Tisza and the Sava. In those sections of the Danube with a very slight drop, such as along the Slovak-Hungarian border, in southern Hungary and northern Croatia, flood-plains are inundated year after year. The flooding has produced a remarkable zone of woods, ponds and streams, now protected as nature reserves and national parks, offering a refuge for richly diversified wildlife.

Iron Gate

The Danube achieves its greatest breadth below Belgrade. Further south, spectacular scenery awaits the voyager, as the river carves a cleft through the Southern Carpathian Mountains at the narrow gorge of the Iron Gate. A hydroelectric power plant was built here in 1971, making a major impact on the natural environment, but at least one positive result was that this stretch of the river, previously feared for its cataracts, became navigable for ships.

What's in a Name? The Donau in Germany and Austria, Duna in Hungary, Dunav to the Serbs, the Croats and the Bulgarians, Dunaj in Slovakia and Dunărea in Romania, the Danube was known as Istros to the ancient Greeks—and is Tuna to the Turks. The name derived from the Latin Danubius, the name of a Roman river god. However, its roots are far older, either from the Celtic or perhaps the Farsi *Danu*, meaning quite simply "to flow" or "to run". This ancient term is at the base of several other European rivers—the Donetsk, the Dniepr, the Don in Russia, and also the English River Don.

From the Iron Gate, the river flows into the lowlands of Walachia, where it is hemmed in on the Bulgarian side by craggy mountain spurs, whilst the opposite, Romanian bank is flat and marshy. The Danube turns northward before reaching the Dobrogea tableland, to turn back eastward at Galaţi. After this final dogleg, the marshy delta region begins.

The People

The Danubian region is a mosaic of diverse peoples. Today's Romanians are proud to claim Dacians and Romans as their ancestors; those of the Bulgarians were Slavs and Thracians. Germans, too, have had an impact on the culture of the region: in the 12th century, King Géza of Hungary brought Saxons into Transylvania, and in the 18th century Archduchess Maria Theresa of Austria settled Swabians on the lower Danube to revitalize and cultivate deserted lands. The political upheavals of the 20th century forced the majority of the descendants of these settlers to return to their former homeland.

The source of the Danube in the castle park of Donaueschingen. | A painterly view of Stein on the bank of the Danube. | The imposing Chain Bridge in Budapest. | Waterlilies in bloom.

Huber/Schmid

istockphoto.com/ene

istockphoto.com/Rus

Passau was built at the confluence of the Danube, the Inn and the Ilz.

Passau Tourismus

FLASHBACK

About 250,000 years ago, *Homo palaeohungaricus*, a primitive form of human being, settled in the middle Danube valley, now Hungary, attracted by the abundance of water and wildlife, and perhaps even by the hot springs that remain a magnet to this day.

Trade along the Danube developed as far back as the Neolithic period (ca. 6000 BC). The Thracians, the original inhabitants of what is now Bulgaria, spread to the lands between the lower Danube and the northern Aegean around 1000 BC. By the 7th century BC, Greek sailors reached the Danube delta and explored upstream, opening the way for commerce.

Celtic tribes established themselves in the valley of the upper Danube, now southern Germany, by 600 BC. They spread eastwards, settling along the middle Danube and its tributary the Sava, and in the 3rd century BC built a fortress on the site of the future Belgrade. Under pressure from the Romans, Germanic tribes from northern Europe and the Iranian-descended Sarmatians, Celtic domination was broken by around 120 BC. In present-day Romania, the Dacian kingdom was born.

Rome Moves In

From 27 BC, under Emperor Augustus, the Romans' conquest of the Danube valley made the river they called the Danubius (and in its lower reaches, the Ister) the empire's northern border. On the other side lived a variety of tribal peoples the Romans labelled barbarians, among them Celts, Pannonians and Illyrians. A line of fortifications (the Limes) was built along the river to repel barbarian incursions. Some 20,000 Roman soldiers were deployed between Vienna and Budapest, and still more along the upper and lower reaches of the river. A Roman fleet patrolled its waters and strongholds were constructed at strategic points on its banks. These quickly grew into flourishing towns, including Castra Regina (Regensburg), Vindobona (Vienna), Aquincum (Budapest), Singidunum (Belgrade) and Sexantaprista (Ruse). Other important riverside fortresses such as

Ratiaria (Vidin) and Nicopolis ad Istrum (Nikopol) were built at the mouths of tributaries.

In AD 106, the expansionist Emperor Trajan defeated the Dacians and so gained control of the entire course of the Danube, as well as extensive lands to the north, roughly the area now covered by Romania and Moldova. His successor Hadrian called a halt to further conquest, in order to concentrate on organizing and defending the vast territories under Roman rule.

In the 3rd century, Goths hailing from north of the Black Sea penetrated southwards to the Danube and crossed it in force. It took a strong Roman army led by the Emperor Gallienus and two future emperors, Claudius II and Aurelian, to defeat them at the battle of Naissus (now Nis in Serbia) in 269. The victory was so complete that it was almost a century before the frontier once again had to be defended against Goths and Sarmatians. Major invasions took place but also relatively peaceful immigration, in which whole tribes fleeing the warlike Huns were allowed to settle within the Empire.

Barbarians and Christians

In the 4th and early 5th centuries, large tribes of Goths and other Germanic peoples moved into the Danubian region and weakened the Roman Empire. Worse was to follow in the 5th century when Huns from the Asian steppes, led by Attila, ravaged southeastern Europe and invaded the Roman heartland of Italy itself.

In the 6th and 7th centuries, the previously little-known Slavs from eastern Europe expanded west and southwards, and in the lands which today form Bulgaria they intermingled with the Thracian population. In the 8th century Charlemagne, Emperor of the Franks, brought much of western and central Europe under his rule, driving out the Goths and the descendants of Attila's Huns. However, Magyars from somewhere between the Volga river and the Ural mountains settled in Hungary along with a lesser number of Turkic Petchenegs.

In the 10th century ten tribes — seven Hungarian Magyars and three Khazar — united to defend themselves from menacing Petchenegs, Russians and Bulgars. Prince Arpád, head of the Magyars, was named supreme leader. Hungary's conversion to Christianity in 975, initiated under a great-grandson of Arpád, Prince Géza, made the Danube a relatively safe overland route for pilgrims going to the Holy Land. Géza's son Stephen was crowned in the year 1000 as the first king of Hungary. Canonized after his death, Stephen became the country's patron saint. The river proved rather more perilous for the huge, disorganized groups of French and Germans who set out in 1096 on the so-called People's Crusade to "save" Jerusalem from Islam. Pillaging their way through Austria and Hungary, they soon antagonized the local people and there were many skirmishes and some full-scale battles. Later crusades however brought something of an economic a boom to the towns along the banks of the Danube. England's King Richard I the Lion-Heart was imprisoned in Dürnstein Castle on his way home from Palestine in 1192. In 1396, in the so-called "Last Crusade", an army of 100,000 Germans, French, Hungarians, Poles, Bohemians, Italians and Spaniards congregated at Budapest and advanced down the Danube—to meet with a crushing defeat by the Turks at Nicopolis, now Nikopol in Bulgaria.

The Viceroy of Hungary, János (John) Hunyadi, repelled Turkish invaders (1456) at Nándorfehérvár (now Belgrade) but died, probably of the plague, in the same year. His eldest son was murdered soon afterwards and his second son Mátyás (Matthias) was chosen by the Hungarian nobles to succeed as king at the age of 15. Renowned as the "just king" Matthias I Corvinus, he

istockphoto.com/?alis

The spectacular ruins of Devin Castle in Slovakia near the border with Austria.

reigned from 1458 to 1490, regarded in Hungary as an intellectual golden age.

The Turkish Tide

In the 16th century, the Danube became the route of a "crusade" in reverse, as Suleiman the Magnificent's Ottoman Turks carried Islam west from the Black Sea. After the battle of Mohács in 1526, Hungary fell to the Ottomans for 150 years. Serbia, Bosnia and parts of Romania also came under their rule. However,

An Orthodox icon in a church in Constanța (Romania).

in spite of besieging it in 1529 and again in 1683, the Ottomans failed to take Vienna, which became the base for Austria's Habsburg rulers to undertake the gradual reconquest of Hungary by 1687, followed by Transylvania in 1691. The Treaty of Karlowitz (Sremski Karlovci) ended the war against the Turks in 1699 and made Austria the major power in the Danube region.

During the reign of Maria Theresa (1740–80), the peoples of most of the Danube region were united. The Archduchess moved German settlers into the areas that had been left deserted after the expulsion of the Turks, and these energetic newcomers introduced new methods of agriculture, developed trade and industry and built whole new villages and towns. The Ottoman Turks were not yet completely beaten; they still held large parts of the Balkans. However, in the Russo-Turkish War of 1768–74 Russia occupied the principalities of Moldavia and Walachia, and thanks to the Treaty of Svištov (1791), Austria gained the Iron Gate pass on the Danube near Orșova. Russia conducted further wars against Turkey, some of them in the Danubian region. In the Treaty of Adrianople (Edirne) in 1829, almost all of the Danube delta was ceded to Russia.

Another important event took place in 1829: the founding of the Donau-Dampfschifffahrtsgesellschaft (Danube Steamship Company). Its operations began with a service linking Vienna and Budapest. Until World War I it was the biggest inland shipping company in the world. Under the terms of the Treaty of Paris (1856) following the Crimean War, Russia lost control of shipping on the lower Danube, which was declared open to international traffic.

In 1877 the Russian Tsar Alexander II launched another war against the Turks, with the declared aim of freeing Bulgaria from their rule. After a five month-long siege and huge loss of life on both sides, the Turkish stronghold of Pleven fell to Russian forces, and in 1878 Bulgaria became an independent state. After 1870 the Danube was rerouted around Vienna to prevent flooding.

The End of an Empire

When World War I came to an end in 1918, the Austro-Hungarian monarchy collapsed; Hungary and Czechoslovakia became independent states, and the new Kingdom of the Serbs, Croats and Slovenes (later to be known as Yugoslavia) united a large part of the Balkans. An international Danube Commission was set up in 1923 to control traffic on the river from Ulm in southern Germany all the way to the Black Sea, and keep navigational equipment in good repair. In 1932 at a conference on Danubian affairs held in London, the French prime minister Tardieu even suggested an economic union of the nations of the Danubian region (although Germany was excluded), a forerunner of the European Union, but his plan failed to gain enough support.

World War II and After

During World War II, the Danube became a battle line. German naval forces used the river to reach the Black Sea. The victorious Soviet army occupied Hungary and Romania in 1944 and marched into Belgrade, although Tito's partisans could take some of the credit for the defeat of the Germans.

In the aftermath of the war, communist regimes were imposed on the nations of Central Europe and the Balkans. Austria was divided into Soviet and western-controlled zones until 1955, when a peace agreement restored its independence as a neutral nation.

The fall of the Berlin Wall in 1989 has had far-reaching consequences for all the nations on the middle and lower Danube. The former Soviet-bloc states threw off the communist yoke, and most succeeded in managing the transition to some form of democracy. The sad exception was Yugoslavia, where nationalist, ethnic and religious tensions led to its break-up and brought chaos and tragedy to many of its people. In 1999, Serbia, the largest of the six separate states that emerged from the wreck, launched an attack on its rebellious province of Kosovo, in defiance of international warnings. In response, NATO forces bombed the Danube bridges in Serbia, closing the river to shipping for some years. With all of them now rebuilt, normal commerce has been resumed, including river cruises all the way to the Black Sea.

Meanwhile, the two-stage enlargement of the European Union to 27 nations has extended its reach along the whole course of the Danube: Hungary and Slovakia joined in 2004, Romania and Bulgaria in 2007.

The Marienberg citadel watches over the River Main at Würzburg.

istockphoto.com / Khiman

ON THE SCENE

A Danube cruise sets its own agenda. Over its entire length, the great river flows through, or past, ten Central and East-European countries. Fields, forests and picturesque villages slip by at a gentle pace. The ship ties up at a succession of charming little towns and great cities, usually close to the historic centres so you can stroll ashore to take in the principal sights.

Würzburg to Passau

Before embarking on the Danube itself, many cruises begin on the River Main, linked to it by canal. Some start at Würzburg, a proud episcopal city straddling the River Main.

Würzburg

The illustrious bishopric lies in the heart of Franconia's wine country. Vineyards spread up the slopes around the Marienberg citadel overlooking the town from across the Main river. This Renaissance fortress houses the Mainfränkisches Museum of regional art and folklore, including ancient wine-presses. But the most cherished works are the Gothic sculptures of Tilman Riemenschneider, who made Würzburg his home from 1483 to 1531.

Residenz

In the episcopal princes' Residenz designed by Balthasar Neumann and Lukas von Hildebrandt (1744), the city possesses one of the finest baroque palaces in Germany. Giambattista Tiepolo painted the Europa fresco over the grand ceremonial staircase, as well as those in the oval Kaisersaal (Imperial Hall) depicting Würzburg's medieval history. Neumann's triumph is the Hofkirche, the court church flooded with light and colour. Tiepolo contributed an Assumption and the Angels' Fall from Heaven for two side altars. Don't miss the candlelit winetastings in the court cellars.

Neumünster

Another fine baroque church is the Neumünster, its noble façade attributed to Johann Dientzenhofer. Inside, a Riemenschneider Madonna in stone stands in the southeast niche of the rotunda. The church is the burial shrine of St Kilian, the Irish missionary martyred in Würzburg in 689. The neighbouring cathedral (rebuilt since destruction in 1945) is dedicated to the monk. On the south side of the transept, several Riemenschneider sculptures are placed in a modern stone setting.

Ochsenfurt

About 20 km (12 miles) upstream from Würzburg you reach Ochsenfurt, whose town walls date back to the 14th century. The old timber framed houses on Hauptstrasse are particularly pretty with their wrought-iron signs. Here you will also find the late-Gothic Rathaus (town hall), one of the finest in Franconia, whose musical clock is the town's emblem. The Andreaskirche (13th–15th centuries) has a richly decorated interior with a sculpture by Riemenschneider. Frankish traditions are upheld in many folklore festivals. King Richard I of England was detained here in 1193, one of several places he was held, while returning to England from the Third Crusade.

Kitzingen

The former importance of Kitzingen, one of the oldest towns on the Main (8th century), is apparent from its Renaissance town hall and several churches dating from the 15th to 18th centuries. Parts of the town walls still remain.

Volkach

The attractive little wine-growing town of Volkach, on a loop of the Main, is worth a visit for its fine Renaissance town hall and the baroque Schelfenhaus, but especially for the pilgrim church of St Maria im Weingarten (St Mary-in-the-Vineyard) to the northwest of the town, which houses Riemenschneider's Rosenkranz-madonna (Madonna of the Rosary).

Schweinfurt

Schweinfurt is the biggest industrial centre of Lower Franconia. The city has been destroyed several times over the centuries, most recently in World War II. Nevertheless, some buildings remain to attest to its historic importance as a free imperial city, among them the late-Romanesque Johanniskirche (altered several times), the town hall (16th century), the former Gymnasium (grammar school), now the town museum, and the Zeughaus (armoury).

Hassfurt

The delightful Franconian town of Hassfurt lies 28 km (17 miles)

Main-Danube Canal. In 1992 the dreams of Charlemagne and Ludwig I of Bavaria were realised when the Main–Danube Canal between Bamberg and Kelheim was completed, opening to seagoing ships a 3,500-km (2,170-mile) waterway linking the North Sea with the Black Sea. Work on the canal began in the Middle Ages. The Ludwigskanal, with 100 locks along its 177 km (110-mile) was inaugurated with great ceremony in 1846, but competition from the railways proved disastrous. Further work was undertaken in 1922, the stretch from Bamberg to Nuremberg became navigable in 1972, and in 1992 the final stretch to Kelheim was inaugurated. The resulting waterway is an engineering marvel, with 16 locks in a total length of 171 km (106 miles).

istockphoto.com/Busto

further on. Its late-Gothic Ritter-kapelle (Knights' Chapel) is embellished by a heraldic frieze with 241 coats of arms, together with interesting tombs. The Gothic Pfarrkirche (parish church) contains several works of art, including a wooden sculpture of John the Baptist by Riemenschneider.

Bamberg

Only 30 km (19 miles) to go until you reach the episcopal city of Bamberg. The old town is graced with works by Riemenschneider and the architect family Dientzenhofer. The picturesque fishing quarter of "Little Venice" (Klein Venedig) lies on the right-hand bank of the river. At the end of August, the old town is the site of an exuberant fair. Along with hearty Franconian dishes you can enjoy a glass of Bamberg's speciality: smoked beer (Rauchbier)!

Cathedral

Take a good look at the cathedral, where the transition from Romanesque to Gothic can be clearly traced. It houses the tomb of Emperor Heinrich II and his wife, a work by Riemenschneider, as well as the Bamberger Reiter, a remarkable Gothic equestrian statue in stone.

Neue Residenz

On Karolinenplatz stand the late-Gothic Alte Hofhaltung (the for-

mer episcopal palace, now housing the historical museum) and the early baroque Neue Hofhaltung (also called the Neue Residenz). The latter, designed by J.L. Dientzenhofer, has on the first floor a gallery of paintings by German masters, and on the second you can admire grand chambers with antique furniture and tapestries. There's a fine view of the old town and the Benedictine abbey of St Michael from the rose garden.

Altes Rathaus
On an island in the River Regnitz, which once separated the castle district from the bourgeois quarter, stands the Altes Rathaus (Old Town Hall), decorated with 18th-century frescoes.

Bayreuth
Make a side-trip to Bayreuth, known for its annual festival of Richard Wagner's operas. The composer's home, **Villa Wahnfried**, is now a museum (closed till 2013) containing stage sets, costumes and musical memorabilia. Wagner is buried in the garden with his wife Cosima, daughter of Liszt. The Markgräfiches Opern-

Wagner's operas find an elegant venue in Bayreuth. | Nuremberg's medieval buildings have been restored. | Traditional costumes in Ochsenfurt.

haus, by two theatre designers from Bologna in the 18th century, is a charming baroque creation, with three galleries festooned in stucco trimmings.

Nuremberg

A fine-looking town, Nuremberg (in German Nürnberg) can once more look with pride on its distinguished history. A centre of medieval culture and veritable heart of Renaissance art north of the Alps, it has also always been at the forefront of German industry and commerce. Today, with a population of 504,000, it dominates the northern Bavarian region of Franconia. Largely destroyed in World War II, it has been lovingly restored, and its churches, museums and culinary delicacies are incentives to spend time here.

Old Town

Near the castle, opposite the Tiergärtner Gate, the **Albrecht Dürer House** was bought by the painter in 1509. He lived there until his death in 1528. This characteristic late-Gothic patrician residence, gabled and half-timbered, has been restored as a museum of the artist's life and work.

Over at Burgstrasse 15, the **Stadtmuseum Fembohaus** (1596) is a magnificent example of Renaissance architecture and craftmanship. Inside, its fine wooden panelling, stucco work and painted ceilings make an appropriate setting for a museum of 16th–19th century domestic life.

Of the city's many ornamental fountains, look out on Rathausgasse for the 16th-century **Gänsemännchen-Brunnen**, depicting a jolly fellow in bronze carrying two geese. His good humour contrasts with the monumental pomp of the Schöner Brunnen on Hauptmarkt, where princes and prophets celebrate the old imperial glories. The marketplace is the setting of the December Nürnberger **Christkindlesmarkt**, a feast of lights, music and the good things of Christmas.

Restored to its former majesty on the market square is the **Frauenkirche**, the stepped-gable 14th-century church destroyed in 1945. Every day at noon, on the huge 16th-century clock at the top of the gabled porch, seven prince-electors come out to honour their emperor, Karl IV. Inside, the outstanding work is the 15th-century Tucher Altar in the north aisle, depicting in its central triptych, by an unknown artist, the Crucifixion, flanked by the Annunciation and Resurrection.

Museums

On the Kornmarkt, the **Germanisches Nationalmuseum** is housed in a Carthusian monastery. Pride of place goes to Albrecht Dürer's paintings, among them his *Lamentation of Christ*.

Germany's oldest stone bridge crosses the Danube at Regensburg and dates back to the 12th century.

At Karlstrasse 13, the **Spielzeug-musem** (Toy Museum) presents a wonderful array of toys and a puppet theatre.

The German Railways' **DB Museum**, at Lessingstrasse 6, displays a replica of Nuremberg's original Adler steam engine of 1835, along with other vehicles of historic interest.

In the Justizpalast, **Courtroom 600, Memorial Nuremberg Trials**, opened end 2010.

Berching

The small Bavarian town greets the visitor with a skyline straight out of the Middle Ages: the town ramparts (constructed around 1450), with 13 towers and four gates, are intact, and you can walk along parts of the walls.

Altmühl Valley

The health resort of **Riedenburg** became a market town in the 13th century, protected by three castles. The valley of the Altmühl is popular with nature lovers, hikers, canoeists and cyclists alike.

The Jagdfalkenhof (Falconry Lodge) at **Schloss Rosenburg** (built 1112) gives daily demonstrations with large birds of prey.

Kelheim

Here the Main–Danube Canal ends and the Altmühl flows into the Danube, which has made its way from its sources in the Black Forest in southwest Germany. The remains of the medieval walls and gates of Kelheim, founded around 1200, can still be seen. Note the Gothic parish church and the elegant façades of the baroque town houses. To the west of Kelheim, the 45-m (147-ft) Befreiungshalle (Liberation Hall), built by Ludwig I of Bavaria to commemorate the wars of liberation fought against Napoleon, crowns the Michelsberg.

Weltenburg

The Benedictine monastery of Weltenburg stands in a setting full of natural drama, where the Danube cuts a narrow gorge through the hills of the Franconian Alb. This is where the Christianization of Bavaria is supposed to have begun in the 7th century. The monastery church, a late-baroque jewel, was built in 1716–18 by the Asam brothers, who were active in south Germany but also further afield in Bohemia and Silesia. Earthly pleasures are catered for by the beer from the monastery-run brewery.

Regensburg

Like Bamberg, Regensburg survived the war almost unscathed, preserving its historical splendour. The city hails back to Roman times, when the mighty Porta Praetoria was built (see vestiges in the north wing of the

ROTHENBURG OB DER TAUBER

This town south of Würzburg is the quintessence of Germany's most romantic era. Medieval ramparts, monumental gates and lofty gabled half-timbered houses, beautifully preserved, recall Rothenburg's past glories. The town is built on heights over a river valley. Serving as a natural moat beneath its western walls, the Tauber river has its source 14 km (8 miles) south of town and joins the Main river 120 km (75 miles) to the north. Begin your walk around town at the 15th-century Ratstrinkstube, now the **Tourist Information Office**, on the north side of Marktplatz. The figures on the old clock go into action on the hour from 11 a.m. to 3 p.m. and from 8 to 10 p.m.

The imposing **Rathaus** is an apt expression of Rothenburg's civic pride during its medieval and Renaissance glory. Anyone tackling the stairs to the top of the 60-m (196-ft) belfry gets a splendid view over the town and Tauber valley. To the east, the Renaissance façade (1572–78) added a fine arcade in 1681.

A 700-year-old Dominican convent houses the **Reichsstadtmuseum**. Its exhibits include the monastic kitchens, medieval and Renaissance furniture, utensils, weapons and interesting memorabilia from the old Jewish community. The Hohenstaufens' castle has long gone, but the **Burgtor** city gate (1360) still stands, leading to the castle gardens with a good view of the Tauber valley.

Bischofshof). The diocese was founded in the 8th century, and from this time princes and emperors held their Diets in the city. Regensburg's heyday was the Middle Ages, and to this day the magnificence of the merchants' houses attests to their wealth and prestige. The **Steinerne Brücke** (Stone Bridge) is the oldest bridge in Germany (12th-century), and connects the main part of the city with the settlement on the opposite bank.

The beautiful old city is dominated by the magnificent Gothic **Petersdom**, with its two 105-m (344-ft) spires. **St Emmeram's Basilica** dates back to the 8th century but has the Asam brothers to thank for its sumptuous baroque interior. The finest secular building in the city is probably the **Old Town Hall**.

Huber/Mehlig

Passau Tourismus

Its feet almost in the water, the monastery at Weltenburg. | The church organ in the Stefansdom at Passau is the biggest in Europe.

Walhalla

A short distance downstream, a huge white marble pseudo-Grecian temple towers above the Danube: this is Walhalla, built for Ludwig I of Bavaria. Climb the 358 steps from the moorings to the temple, which houses busts of eminent Germans.

Straubing

Straubing lies in the fertile Dungau, the heart of the Bavarian granary. In the picturesque Altstadt (Old Town), see the 14th-century Stadtturm with its five spires on Hauptplatz; Theresienplatz and Ludwigsplatz are surrounded by patrician houses. One of the finest churches is the Ursulinenkirche, designed by the Asam brothers. A short distance out of town, the Peterskirche is Straubing's oldest place of worship, built around 1180. One of the churchyard's three chapels is devoted to Agnes Bernauer, a barber's daughter who was drowned as a witch in the Danube.

The Danube traces a hairpin loop at Schlögen.

Huber/Gräfenhain

Passau to Vienna

The "Town of Three Rivers", Passau, stands at the confluence of the Danube, the Inn joining it from the south and the little Ilz from the north. Champions of the Inn (which gives its name to Innsbruck) note that it is broader and bluer here than the Danube, and so much more deserving of Johann Strauss's waltz. Ships moor below the proud Veste Oberhaus castle, and Austria is but a stone's throw away.

Passau

On the German side of the border, Passau (km 2227) is a solid old bishopric that has always enjoyed the good life, celebrating its religious festivities with plenty of music, beer for the men and hot chocolate for the ladies. Historically prospering from trade in wine, wheat and salt, it is an inviting city, from the bulbous onion domes and graceful arches of its baroque monuments to the rounded promontories separating the waterways.

Burg Oberhaus

For a fine view over the town's charming backdrop of green wooded hillsides, make your way up to the Oberhaus fortress. The castle museum offers a good introduction to the life and times of the region's medieval inhabitants and their crafts — of old, Passau rivalled Damascus and Toledo for the delicate workmanship of its finely honed sword blades.

Stephansdom

To the south, the core of the town stands on the ridge of land between the Danube and Inn rivers. Towering over it is the cathedral of St Stephan, with its three onion domes, Flamboyant Gothic chancel, rich baroque interior boasting a total of 1,000 sculpted figures, and Europe's biggest church organ, with 17,774 pipes.

Through the Mühl Region

At **Lindau** (km 2222), where more Danube cruise ships dock on the German left bank, as far as the

---

Passau's pacifists. The people of Passau have always been far too fond of the good life to spoil it by wasting time fighting. When the town was besieged by the Bavarians in 1703, the bishop's three companies of soldiers declined to report for duty, explaining that they had all come down with a fever. The Bavarian forces were eventually able to complete their conquest, but not until 1741 — and their general, much frustrated, complained that he had met no opposition at all!

Jochenstein power station (lock at km 2203), the river forms the German-Austrian border. For the next 323 km, it flows through Austria, at first through the wooded hill country of the Upper Austrian Mühlviertel. River travellers are charmed here by medieval villages, knights' castles, monasteries and the splendid narrow loop of the **Schlögener Schlinge** (km 2187).

The hydroelectric power stations of Aschach (km 2162) and Ottensheim-Wilhering (km 2147) oblige ships to pass once more through locks.

Linz

Standing where the Danube valley flattens into a plain, Linz (km 2135), capital of the province of Upper Austria, rises from the banks of the river at an important communications junction with Germany and the Czech Republic. The first (horsedrawn) railroad on the continent was inaugurated in Linz in 1832, running to Budweis in Bohemia, and five years later the first Danube steamships arrived, encouraging the expansion of the mining, metal, machine and textile industries. Post-war, the city concentrated on heavy industry and chemicals. In the 1990s a congress and trade fair centre was built, as well as the Ars Electronica Center. The huge Voestalpine steel plant is located across the Nibelung Bridge on the north bank, along with important chemical factories. The port, separated from the river by a protective harbour with special wharves, is Austria's biggest, handling 5 million tonnes of goods per year.

In the past, countless scholars, poets, musicians and architects found the town a most congenial place to put down roots: Mozart and Beethoven stopped here long enough to write the Linz Symphony and the 8th respectively. Linz was designated a European Capital of Culture for 2009.

Hauptplatz

The heart of the remarkably well-preserved Old Town (Altstadt) on Linz's south bank centres around the Hauptplatz, with its stately pastel-coloured buildings from the 17th and 18th centuries and an imposing Gothic Rathaus (city hall). The magnificent baroque Jesuitenkirche cathedral (or Alter Dom) is where composer Anton Bruckner (1824–96) served as organist. In the middle of the square juts the white-marble Trinity Column (Dreifaltigkeitssäule) of thanksgiving erected in 1723. A carillon plays several times a day. A short walk away, the **Lentos Kunstmuseum** displays artworks of the 19th and 20th centuries.

Landhaus

The Landhaus, a few steps away on Klosterstrasse, is a gracious Renaissance palace with arcaded courtyard and flower-bedecked balconies. Its fountain depicts the planets, recalling that the great German astronomer Johannes Kepler taught in this building in the 17th century, when it was a university. Today it houses the provincial government.

Schlossmuseum

The ancient castle on the Danube, one of the residences of the Emperor Friedrich III, is one of

SALZBURG

A golden city, home of Mozart and echoing to a thousand other musical themes, Salzburg lies in an unequalled environment of mountains, hills and forest, along the banks of the River Salzach. Some 100 km (62 miles) south of Linz, it is a popular excursion for cruise passengers.

There is something indefinably southern about the old part of town, which many compare with Florence or Venice. Baroque architecture gives it a dreamy, poetic charm. Narrow streets lead into spacious squares, elegant settings for Gothic churches and monasteries and ornately sculpted fountains. Mansions and Renaissance palaces reign over beautiful parks and gardens. Today Salzburg is entirely pervaded by Mozart. Recitals are held in the most splendid ceremonial rooms of the palaces and castles; his homes are preserved as museums. There's the Mozarteum music academy, the annual festival, and even chocolates, Mozartkugeln. The 250th anniversary of his birth in 2006 was marked by a host of events and celebrations.

A good place to start exploring is the heart of the Old Town. In the centre of **Residenzplatz** stands a large baroque fountain (1658–61) surrounded by splendid rearing horses. At 7 and 11 a.m., and 6 p.m., familiar melodies by Mozart ring out on the 35 bells of the 17th-century Glockenspiel, on the east side of the square. The west side is taken up by the Residenz, a palace of the archbishops founded in 1120 (the present buildings date from the 17th and 18th centuries). The south side of Residenzplatz is dominated by the huge **Dom** (Cathedral). It was built in Italian Renaissance style, with baroque overtones, between 1614 and 1655. In the first side chapel to the left of the entrance, is the Romanesque font, supported by four bronze lions, where the baby Mozart was christened in 1756.

The **Rupertinum**, a 17th-century palace built by Paris Lodron, houses the museum of modern art (Museum der Moderne). The works by Kokoschka, Kirchner, Nolde and Egon Schiele are particularly noteworthy.

Backing into the base of the Mönchsberg, the long building of the **Festspielhaus** (Festival Hall) has been converted from the former court stables. It includes several theatres, the Haus für Mozart and other concert halls, and a riding school with three rows of seats carved out of the hillside. The 130 horses that were quartered in these palatial lodgings had the exclusive rights to the waters of the **Pferde-schwemme** on nearby Sigmunds-platz. A grandiose Renaissance structure of 1695, this splendid horse trough is ornamented with frescoes of prancing steeds, dominated by a vigorous sculpted group by Michael Bernhard Mandl depicting a man breaking in a horse.

Getreidegasse is the great shopping street of Salzburg's old town. A veritable forest of wrought-iron guild signs adorns its Renaissance and baroque façades. The houses are narrow but four or five storeys high and delving deep on each side, around alleyways and hidden courtyards (at, for example, Nos. 23, 25, 34 and 38). Number 9 is **Mozart's birthplace**—now an enchanting museum. Exhibits include manuscripts of minuets Mozart wrote when he was five, his counterpoint notebook, paintings of papa Leopold and sister Nannerl. A clavichord bears a note written by wife Constanze: "On this piano my dear departed husband Mozart composed *The Magic Flute*".

Getreidegasse opens onto Rathausplatz; continue past the Town Hall to the **Alter Markt** on your right. At No. 6, don't miss the pharmacy (Hofapotheke) that has kept its old rococo décor.

At No. 8, Makartplatz, Mozart's Residence, the **Tanzmeisterhaus**, was the family home from 1773 to 1780. It has been converted into a Mozart museum displaying his personal fortepiano.

Trinity Church, with a concave façade, is another of Fischer van Erlach's baroque masterpieces (1694–1702). The large building on the west side of the square is the State Theatre: behind it is the Marionettentheater where puppets perform *The Magic Flute*. The Mozarteum next door is the Academy of Music.

Corbis/Bianchetti

SALZKAMMERGUT

A popular round-trip east of Salzburg takes you to the lakes and spas of the Salzkammergut. On the shore of a crescent-shaped lake beneath the steep slopes of the Drachenwand and Schafberg mountains, the town of **Mondsee** grew up around a 15th-century Benedictine abbey. Some of its buildings serve as a museum recounting the life of the neolithic inhabitants of the lake region. At the southern tip of the Mondsee, a succession of tunnels and narrow roads overhung by rocks form a pass between Scharfling and St Gilgen, on **Wolfgangsee**. Mozart's mother was born in **St Gilgen**, a resort prized for its water sports facilities. You can take a paddle-steamer from here to the town of **St Wolfgang**. A place of pilgrimage since the 12th century, St Wolfgang's church has a fine altarpiece by Michael Pacher, completed in 1481, depicting the coronation of the Virgin. The famous White Horse Inn *(Weisses Rössl)* set to music by Ralph Benatzky is here, on the lakefront. East of St Wolfgang, **Bad Ischl** was one of Europe's greatest cultural centres during the reign of Franz-Joseph, who spent his summers here hunting and taking the waters. In his wake came all the big names of the 19th-century art and music world: Johann Strauss, Brahms, Franz Lehar, Nestroy, Anton Bruckner, and so on. Today you can visit the emperor's villa (Kaiservilla). Empress Sissi preferred the little marble castle (Marmorschlössl) in the park, now a photography museum. South of Bad Ischl, **Hallstatt** is one of the most picturesque of Austrian villages, a cluster of white houses squeezed between the dark lake and the wooded slopes of the Dachstein. Its salt was extracted as far back as neolithic times, as you will learn in the local museum. North of Bad Ischl, the road through the **Traun valley** was one of the great European salt routes. The section between Ebensee and Traunkirchen is hewn into the rock high above the **Traunsee**, Austria's deepest lake. At its northern end, the town of **Gmunden** has an island castle linked to the shore by a wooden walkway. The scenic route back to Salzburg takes you across to **Steinbach am Attersee** then follows the east shore of the lake. Make a halt at the lookout point at **Buchberg**.

several Upper Austria museums (Landesmuseen). Its very modern south wing opened in 2009. The collections include Applied Arts, coins, weapons, musical instruments (with a piano played by Beethoven) and medieval artworks. The nearby Carolingian **Martinskirche** is the oldest church in Austria to retain most of its original 8th-century form.

The Lentos-Kunstmuseum at Linz is housed in a modern building on the right bank.

Pöstlingberg

For a good view of the city, the surrounding countryside and the Alps, cross the river to the north bank, where a steep electric railway climbs to the top of the Pöstlingberg.

Linz to Mauthausen

Beyond the extensive Linz harbour and river mouth of the Traun come the locks at the Abwinden-Asten power plant (km 2120).

Mauthausen (km 2112), originally established as an imperial customs station at the confluence with the Enns river, is now more bitterly remembered as the site of Austria's largest concentration camp. A chapel and a monument remember its 100,000 victims.

Just 17 km further, there are more locks at the Wallsee-Mitterkirchen power plant.

Grein

The castle of Greinburg watches over the enchanting town (km 2079), which has a lovely rococo theatre in the main square, which has remained unaltered since it was built in 1790. Werfenburg castle in Struden (km 2076) and the picturesque ruin of Freyenstein on the right bank (km 2070) are also worth a look.

Strudengau and Nibelungengau

After the quite craggy and once dangerous Strudengau stretch of river between Dornach and Persenbeug (km 2060), a baroque castle of the Habsburgs stands on the left bank near the locks of the Ybbs-Persenbeug hydroelectric station. This is the start of one of the Danube's most romantic sections. For 24 km, it flows through the Nibelung region, scene of the song saga that inspired Wagner's operas. The baroque church of **Maria Taferl** above Marbach (km 2050) is the most important pilgrimage church in Lower Austria.

Wachau

The locks of the Melk power station (km 2038) herald the beginning of the Wachau, a UNESCO World Heritage Site since the year 2000. Here the Danube is capable of conjuring up dreamy thoughts in the hardiest of folk as it winds its way just 30 km (19 miles) between Melk and Krems in Lower Austria (Niederösterreich), where country villages alternate with dark castle ruins on craggy cliffs. This stretch basks in an exceptionally mild climate. The best times to see it are spring and autumn.

The Wachau is easily accessible from Vienna by road—90 km (56 miles) on the motorway—or by Danube steamship. Until 1972, when a bridge was built over the Danube near Melk, the only way to cross was by ferry.

Melk

Long before Melk (km 2036) became the home of the Benedictines in 1089, its clifftop position above the river bend made it an ideal military camp from which to fend off barbarians. Melk was settled permanently as early as the 9th century, and the Babenbergs made it their royal residence and stronghold in the 10th, although it was not to receive a charter until 1898.

In the Middle Ages, the salt, wine and iron trades flourished here, their products carried by Danube shipping. In 1548 a fire reduced the town virtually to ashes, and it was rebuilt in the Renaissance style.

Stift Melk

Having crossed the forecourt, you find yourself confronted by the impressive eastern façade of the monastery. This dates from the early 18th century, when Jakob Prandtauer was commissioned to transform the forbidding strategic fortification into a splendid baroque sanctuary with gracefully tapering towers and a majestic octagonal dome. The project was completed after his death by his pupil Josef Munggenast.

The **Marmorsaal** (Marble Hall), light, bright and richly decorated with ceiling frescoes and other ornaments, was used as a dining room and guest room in former days. Pass through the balconies overlooking the Danube to the **Bibliothek**, its magnificent inlaid shelves weighed down with some 100,000 precious books and 2000 manuscripts. The room is a precious work of art in its own right.

A spiral staircase leads down into the **Stiftskirche** (Abbey Church), where you can admire the high altar, the pulpit, the beautifully carved confessionals and choir stalls, the ceiling frescoes by Johann Michael Rottmayr and the great organ.

The treasury includes the **Cross of Melk** inlaid with pearls and precious stones. It is claimed that the cross was stolen in the 12th century. It found its way back to the monastery by mysterious means —floating against the current upstream from Vienna! It can be seen on special occasions.

Between Melk and Dürnstein
Schloss Schönbühel stands on a rock on the right bank (km 2032). The medieval **Aggstein** robber barons' castle is perched in ruin on a rugged hilltop (km 2025). Across the river in **Willendorf** (km 2024) the famous "Venus of Willendorf" fertility statue was found (you can see her in the Naturhistorisches Museum in Vienna). The attractive wine village of **Spitz** (km 2019) awaits with its Hinterhaus medieval castle. The parish church at Weissenkirchen, surrounded by vineyards, combines fortifications with a house of worship (km 2013).

Dürnstein
This pretty little baroque town (km 2009) nestles on the bank of the Danube and can only be explored on foot: cars must be left on the edge of town.

Melk abbey and the ornate ceiling of its Marble Hall. | The banks of the Danube are popular with cyclists.

istockphoto.com/anzeletti

Frédérique Fasser

istockphoto.com/Frank

Kuenringerburg

Dürnstein is famous mainly for the castle above the town in which Richard I of England, the Lion-Heart, was held captive in 1192. He had offended the Babenberg Duke Leopold V during the Third Crusade, and was recognized and captured in Vienna whilst attempting to slip away up the Danube valley. According to the legend, his faithful minstrel Blondel traced him here to Dürnstein by singing the king's favourite songs outside every castle until he came to the right one and heard Richard join in the chorus, but the captive was only released after the payment of a huge ransom; it cost England 23,000 kg of silver. In 1645, during the Thirty Years' War, Swedish troops burned Dürnstein, leaving the Kuenringerburg in ruins. The 20-minute ascent to the castle is rewarded with fine views of the river.

Stiftskirche

The Abbey Church, resplendent in blue and white, has one of the finest baroque towers in the whole of Austria. Walk through the ornate portal and the quiet courtyard to reach the interior, where the three divine virtues Faith, Hope and Charity watch over the carved pulpit. The cloister is worth a visit.

Hauptstrasse

On Hauptstrasse, bounded to the east by the Kremser Tor, you can see many pretty town houses from the 16th to 18th centuries, some of them with sgraffito decoration. On the same street, you will find the late-Gothic **Rathaus**

(town hall) with its fine court-yard. Only ruins remain of the former Klarissenkloster (Convent of the Poor Clares).

Kellerschlössl

You can take part in a wine tasting in the Kellerschlössl (1715), with its huge old wine cellar and rich decoration of frescoes and reliefs.

Krems

The centre of the Wachau's wine industry, Krems (km 2002), linked to Stein by the appropriately named village of Und ("and" in German), is considered to be the most beautiful town in Lower Austria. The three towns have merged into one.

If you walk along Untere Landstrasse, past the Kleines Sgraffitohaus, you will come to the **Simandlbrunnen** ("Simon's Fountain), depicting the character in question returning home from an evening's drinking to a none-too-gentle reception from his angry wife.

Cross Wegscheid to reach Hoher Markt, the town's oldest square. Here stands the resplendent Gothic **Gozzoburg**, a patrician residence built in the 13th century in Italian style by the municipal judge Gozzo.

In the **Piaristenkirche**, the church in Piaristengasse, there's an extensive collection of paintings by Martin Johann Schmidt (1718–1801), a prolific artist familiarly known as Kremser Schmidt, who adorned most of the region's churches.

The **Pfarrkirche** St Veit (St Vitus parish church) is a fine 18th century baroque building decorated

by eminent artists. The large ceiling frescoes and the All Souls Altar, at the back of the church and to the right, are by Kremser Schmidt.

The Dominican church and its adjacent monastic buildings today house the WEINSTADTmuseum, which traces the development of wine-production and the town's history, including a scale model. Exhibitions, conferences and concerts are held in the early Gothic interior of the medieval church.

The Stein Gate at the end of Obere Landstrasse, was part of the medieval city wall. Its round Gothic towers date from the 15th century. But for many, the most enjoyable monuments in Krems are the Renaissance houses on Obere Landstrasse, where they serve the new Heuriger wine in tree-shaded courtyards.

Stein

In Stein, several fine buildings face Steiner Landstrasse. The Minoritenkirche or Minorites' Church was built during the transition from Romanesque to Gothic, and this stylistic blend gives the building its particular character. The Pfarrhof (presbytery), with its fine rococo stucco work, is also worth a visit. The mighty seven-storey tower of the Frauenbergkirche rises above the town.

Stift Göttweig

Visible from far away, Stift Göttweig looks almost unreal sitting on its hill 425 m high a few kilometres south of the Danube. This important Benedictine monastery was founded in the 11th century and rebuilt in baroque style in the 18th century.

Tulln Basin

Ships pass through locks at the hydroelectric works of Altenwörth (km 1980) and Greifenstein (km 1949). Following a popular referendum in 1979, the nuclear power station at Zwentendorf (km 1977) was not linked up to the national power grid. The town of Tulln (km 1963) was once the Roman cavalry post of Compagna, later an important medieval trade centre.

Klosterneuburg

The Augustine abbey at Klosterneuburg (km 1939) was founded in 1114 and rebuilt by Emperor Karl VI in the 18th century to emulate the Escorial in Madrid, home of his Spanish Habsburg ancestors. His dream of a vast baroque palace-cum-church with nine domes, each graced with a Habsburg crown, had to stop short at one big dome, with the imperial crown, and one little one, with the crown of the Austrian archduke. The major attraction of the interior is the

Leopold Chapel's superb 12th-century Verdun Altar with its 45 Biblical scenes painted in enamel panels. As in Krems, the other attraction is outside, in the wine gardens set amid the vineyards at the edge of the Wienerwald (Vienna Woods).

Danube Canal and UNO-City

At km 1934, the narrow Danube Canal forks off towards the Vienna city centre (Innenstadt), but heavy river traffic stays on the main river. The city's striking modern landmarks south of the Vienna Woods—the round **Millennium Tower** (km 1932) on the right bank and the UNO-City complex (km 1929) beyond the artificial Danube Island on the left bank—rise up until you reach the landing stages near the Reichsbrücke (km 1928).

Vienna

The population of Vienna (km 1929), Austria's capital, reflects the cosmopolitan mix of peoples once ruled by the Habsburg Empire: Hungarians, Germans, Czechs, Slovaks, Poles, Spaniards, Flemings and Italians. They have all made a contribution to the city's architecture, music and painting, but also to the cuisine of its restaurants and cafés.

Stephansdom

With its Romanesque western façade, Gothic tower and baroque altars, the cathedral is a marvellous example of the Viennese genius for harmonious compromise, melding the austerity, dignity and exuberance of those great architectural styles.

From the north tower you have a fine view of the city, and of the

Renata Holzbachová

Wien Tourismus/MAXUM

Österreich Werbung

huge Pummerin bell cast from melted-down Turkish cannons after the 1683 siege was repelled. The present bell is a recast version of the original destroyed during World War II.

Mozarthaus Vienna

At Domgasse No. 5, from 1784 to 1787, lived Wolfgang Amadeus Mozart. The modest building (sometimes called Figarohaus) was renovated to re-open on January 27, 2006 for the 250th anniversary of Mozart's birth. He wrote 11 of his piano concertos here, as well as the *Marriage of Figaro* and many other pieces.

Kärntner Strasse, Ring

Stroll back to Kärntner Strasse, the city's main north-south thoroughfare where many of Vienna's smartest shops can be found. It leads past the world-famous **Staatsoper** to the Ring. This boulevard encircling the Innere Stadt was mapped out in the 1860s along the ramparts. Along it are handsome buildings such as the neo-Gothic **Votivkirche**, the **University** and **Rathaus** (Town Hall). On the Innere Stadt side is the **Burgtheater**, a high temple of the Ger-

Schloss Schönbrunn put into in perspective. | Social life in winter is ruled by glamorous balls. | Distinguished members of the Spanish Riding School.

Sissi: myth and reality. Empress Elisabeth (1837–98) was an intelligent and cultivated woman who worried little about court etiquette and much about the destiny of the Hungarian people. After her marriage to her cousin Franz Joseph at the age of 16, she had to exchange a hitherto fairly free life in Bavaria for the strict supervision of her mother-in-law, Sophie. The empress fell ill, probably with a venereal disease acquired from her husband, and took refuge in the milder climate of Madeira— the first of a long series of journeys abroad. In June 1867, the imperial couple were crowned King and Queen of Hungary: the dual monarchy was born. Even this, however, did not keep Sissi in the palace. After she had given her husband four children, she decided at 40 to distance herself still further from court and pursue her passion for poetry and travel. The empress suffered a terrible blow in 1889 when her son, Rudolf, apparently committed suicide on the royal estate of Mayerling, along with his mistress, Baroness Maria Vetsera. Nine years later, when out walking on the Quai du Mont-Blanc in Geneva, Elisabeth was stabbed to death by the Italian anarchist Luigi Lucheni.

man stage. Beyond it is the lovely **Volksgarten**.

From the Staatsoper, walk northwards to Albertinaplatz and on to the Hofburg.

The Hofburg

The most imposing of the imperial palaces is the Hofburg, home of Austria's rulers since the 13th century. Take the guided tour of the **Kaiserappartements**, entrance on Michaelerplatz. Some rooms of the Imperial Apartments now comprise the **Sissi Museum**.

The **Burgkapelle** (Castle Chapel), tucked away in the northern corner of the Schweizerhof, was built in 1449. The Vienna Boys' Choir (Wiener Sängerknaben) sings Mass here every Sunday morning, except in July and August.

In the **Spanische Reitschule** (Spanish Riding School), white Lippizaner horses are trained to walk and dance with a delicacy that many ballet-dancers might envy.

Schönbrunn

Schönbrunn is the smiling, serene expression of the personality of one woman—Maria Theresa, Archduchess of Austria, Queen of Bohemia and Hungary. (You will

The Vienna Philharmonic Orchestra's New Year concert is always a resounding success.

Österreich Werbung

notice that the German spelling of her name is Theresia.)

Visit the gardens first. The park, laid out in the classical French manner, is dominated by the **Gloriette**, a neoclassical colonnade perched on the crest of a hill. In the palace itself, a guided grand tour (audioguides also available) will give you a glimpse of the sumptuous comfort in which Maria Theresa and her successors handled the affairs of state. A short tour takes in only the appartments of Franz-Josef and Sissi in the right wing.

Museums
Vienna's National Gallery, the **Kunsthistorisches Museum**, is outstanding. The **Naturhistorische Museum**, opposite, has zoological, anthropological and paleontological displays, and a beautiful collection of gemstones. Nearby, the modern **MuseumsQuartier** is one of the 10 biggest cultural complexes in the world, with museums, theatres and exhibition halls. The nearby Albertina displays a rich collection of works by Da Vinci, Dürer, Raphael, Rubens, Rembrandt, Klimt and Schiele.

Austrian art is displayed in three different galleries of the **Schloss Belvedere**: medieval art, the baroque museum, and the gallery of 19th and 20th century art, with works by Klimt, Schiele, Kokoschka, Munch and others.

There are museums devoted to Schubert, Haydn, Beethoven and Sigmund Freud. Vienna-born painter and architect Hundertwasser designed the **Kunst Haus Wien – Museum Hundertwasser**, on Untere Weissgerberstr. 13 in the 3rd district, using recycled material and ceramics. The museum displays a collection of the artist's works. The **Hundertwasserhaus** on Löwengasse is a shining example of non-conformism and respect for the environment.

Gumpoldskirchen
South of Vienna lies Gumpoldskirchen, one of the region's most charming wine-growing villages. Be sure to visit the 16th-century Rathaus, the Gothic church and local inns offering the new wine, "Heuriger".

Heiligenkreuz
The Cistercian abbey of Heiligenkreuz southwest of Vienna was founded in the 12th century. The Plague Column (Pestsäule) in the courtyard and the skilfully carved choir stalls are by the baroque artist Giuliani. The cloister, with its red marble pillars, exudes peace and harmony.

Mayerling
Nearby Mayerling achieved its claim to fame through a tragic event: the 30-year-old Crown Prince Rudolf and 17-year-old

Gustav Klimt. Klimt (1862–1918) was a pioneer of modern painting in Vienna. In 1897 he became first president of the Secession group, which gathered several young artists in search of new means of expression. Having assimilated the innovative ideas and spirit of the Impressionists, Symbolists and Pre-Raphaelites, as well as the precepts of Art Nouveau, he developed a powerful personal style, at once opulent and disquieting. Among his major works, one version of *The Kiss* is displayed at the Belvedere, while his 34-m-long Beethoven frieze can be seen in the basement of the Secession pavilion.

Österreichische Galerie Belvedere Wien

Hungarian countess Maria Vetsera were found dead together in the hunting lodge—their relationship had been condemned as scandalous, and Rudolf had been refused a divorce. Emperor Franz Josef had a convent built on the spot where the couple died, and Maria Vetsera was buried in the cemetery of Heiligenkreuz, while Rudolf was laid to rest in the family tomb in Vienna.

Wien-Freudenau

Just before confluence of the Danube Canal, the Danube vessels pass the Wien-Freudenau Locks at km 1921—at the most recent and last of the nine Austrian hydroelectric stations on the Danube, opened in 1997. A much greater energy-creation project was planned further downstream in the 1980s. This would have flooded the riverbanks and destroyed the woodlands with their abundant wildlife and flora. In 1984 thousands of nature-lovers protested and succeeded since 1996 in protecting as the **Donau-Auen National Park** the last 40 km of the natural incline of the Danube as far as the mouth of the River Morava.

Petronell-Carnuntum

Some 2,000 years ago, in the region of Petronell-Carnuntum (km 1890), the Roman fort of Carnuntum was built on a site overlooking the Danube, at the frontier of the Roman Empire near the crossroads of ancient European trade routes. It was also conveniently sited for the Romans to go to the sulphur baths of what is today **Bad Deutsch-Altenburg** (km 1887) on the Hundsheim mountainside.

Hainburg

Hainburg (km 1884) likes to call itself Haydn-Stadt because the great composer, born in nearby Rohrau, went to school here. Medieval castle ruins and town gates recall Hainburg's former significance at the crossroads of trade routes.

The narrow passage at the Danube is known as Hainburg Gate, and shortly after it, on the left bank, is the mouth of the Morava (km 1880), flowing from a deep valley to mark the Austro-Slovak border. For thousands of years this gateway to the Carpathian mountains was a source of constant conflict. Both rivers were guarded by the **Devín Castle** from the time of the Celts to the 17th century. The ruin on the Slovak side is one of the Danube's most picturesque. The present day border, since 2004 an interior frontier of the EU, continues 7 km from the confluence downstream on the Danube and turns off to the south.

Friedensreich Hundertwasser (1928–2000). Christened Friedrich Stowasser, he altered his name to Friedensreich Hundertwasser ("Rich in Peace Hundredwater") in 1949, after three months at Vienna's Academy of Fine Arts—his only formal artistic training. Taking his inspiration from nature, the changing patterns reflected in water, the rhythms of Arabic music, he favoured the use of vibrant, saturated primary colours, and was particularly fascinated by the spiral, albeit an irregular, meandering spiral. His aversion for regular, planned architecture with strict, straight lines led him to design buildings topped with trees and houses with grass roofs, uneven floors and curving walls.

Renata Holzbachová

Window above the entrance to Bratislava's Old Town Hall.

Jean-Paul Minder

Bratislava to Mohács

The new Danube–Oder canal links Bratislava to trade with Poland and eastern Germany. Today its textile, chemical, oil and metal industries are offset by pleasant forests, vineyards and farmland surrounding a handsome baroque city centre.

Bratislava

Capital of Slovakia, Bratislava (km 1869) commands a key position close to Austria and Hungary. Towering over it is the royal castle. The German Pressburg, Hungarian Pozsony and Slovakian Bratislava are in fact one and the same place, its successive names testifying to a rich and varied past.

Castle (Hrad)

Visible from afar, this majestic building with its four corner towers stands prominently on a hill above the Danube, gleaming white after a recent renovation. The fortress dates back to the 9th century, but alterations took place in the 17th and 18th centuries and it is now largely Renaissance in style. It was destroyed by fire in 1811 and rebuilt only after 1953. Those rooms accessible to the public hold part of the collections of the Slovakian National Museum, the Treasury and an exhibition which illustrates the history of the castle and of Slovakia and the music museum .The **Castle Gardens** offer a breathtaking view of the Old Quarter and the Danube.

Also revealing is the view across the river over **Petržalka**, a suburb of housing prefabricated with concrete slabs, erected during the Communist era for over 100,000 people. It borders on Austria, whose green hills of Hainburg are visible from here.

Old Quarter

Leave the gardens by the Gothic **Corvinus Gate**, and descend the Castle Steps to the Old Quarter. Beblavého Street boasts the finest rococo building in the city: the narrow **House of the Good Shepherd**, where you'll find an interesting clock museum.

St Martin's Cathedral

Diagonally opposite on the expressway (use the subway!), you'll see the 14th-century St Martin's Cathedral, one of the most beautiful examples of Gothic architecture in the whole of Slovakia. Between 1563 and 1830, 11 Hungarian monarchs (including Maria Theresa) and their consorts were crowned here, a fact commemorated by the golden crown topping the spire.

Main Square

From the cathedral, take the pretty route along Panská Street, lined with neat Renaissance and baroque palaces, to the Main Square. Of particular interest is the **Old Town Hall** (1325) on the eastern side. The building houses the collections of the **City Museum** (Mestské Múzeum).

Primate's Palace

Heading northeast, you will soon see the neoclassical Primate's Palace, built at the end of the 18th century. In its Mirror Hall, Napoleon and Emperor Franz I of Austria signed the Treaty of Pressburg after the crushing French victory at the Battle of Austerlitz. Part of the art collection of the City Gallery can be found here.

St Michael's Gate

Heading west, you come to the gate, part of the former fortifications of the city. The tower, now 51 m (167 ft) high, has grown since it was first built at the beginning of the 14th century. In 1758 the tower was crowned with a baroque cupola, upon which St Michael sits enthroned. From the top, you have a fine view of the old town.

Theatre and Museums

Major theatres, museums and hotels are grouped in the elegant district between the Danube (Dunaj) and the greenery of wide Hviezdoslavovo Square. At its eastern end stands the Slovak **National Theatre**, built in 1886 in neo-Renaissance style. An impressive new extension stands beside the Danube, east of the old town. The nearby **Reduta Palace**, the home of the Slovak Philharmonic Orchestra, is undergoing renovation.

Directly on the bank of the Danube, you'll find the **Slovak National Gallery** with older and contemporary art, and the **Slovak National Museum** displaying botanical, mineralogical and other exhibits.

Danube Bridge, Nový Most
The modern cable-stayed Danube bridge is surmounted by a single 86-m (282-ft) column with a panoramic restaurant on top.

Gabčikovo Canal
The Danube flows only 23 km through Slovakia between Austria and Hungary before serving, from km 1850, as the Slovak-Hungarian frontier river. Then, however, for a stretch of 38 km, the Danube ships leave the main river just beyond Bratislava at km 1853 to navigate the Gabčikovo Canal, 500 m wide and protected on both sides by tall dikes, flowing through Slovak territory. On a spur of land at Čunovo, where canal and river part, you sail past art works—an open-air exhibition of sculptures from the modern **Danubiana Meulensteen Art Museum**, a circular building also to be seen on the river bank.

Bratislava Castle. | Oops! Watch your step! (artwork in Bratislava). | Statue of Maria Theresa on Europa Square in Komárno, Nitra, Slovakia.

Two smaller arms of the Danube create giant island landscapes in the plain on either side of the main river and the canal. In the north, the Malý Dunaj (Little Danube) embraces the 80 km long Žitný ostrov (Big Debris Island) on Slovak territory, in the south on Hungarian territory, the Mosoni Duna (Mosoni Danube) flows around the 50 km long Szigetköz (Small Debris Island). The many serpentine river branches and dead arms of the river with their woody marshland shelter a significant amount of birdlife.

Some 28 km further on, the canal water is dammed at the Gabčikovo hydroelectric plant. Slovakia produces here about one tenth of its electrical energy needs. Providing a height of fall of over 20 m, the highest locks on the whole Danube were opened here in 1992. The regulation of the Danube at this point protects the hinterland from flooding and guarantees controlled water levels for ship traffic. But as more than three-quarters of the Danube water flows here through the canal, the rest of the Danube lowlands suffer occasionally from a

Basilica of Esztergom. | **Time-faded splendour on the Danube bank at Esztergom.** | **Embroidered costumes are worn for folklore shows.**

Gödöllő. Some 30 km northeast of Budapest, the town of Gödöllő is particularly well-known for its huge and handsome baroque castle. It was built from 1744 to 1748 by by Andreas Mayerhoffer for Count Antal Grassalkovich I (1694–1771). In 1867, when the emperor Franz Joseph I of Austria and his wife Elisabeth (Sissi) were crowned King and Queen of Hungary, they received it as a wedding gift.

The royal pair's regular visits gave the region a new significance. The empress came often, delighted to escape from the stiff etiquette of Vienna and to practise her favourite sport, horse riding. After her death a memorial park was built.

The castle was renovated and opened to the public in 1997. Tours include the state rooms, the park and the stables.

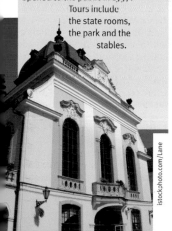

istockphoto.com/Lane

water shortage, threatening gradually to dry out extensive natural woodland marshes. Some 10 km downstream, the canal joins the main river again at km 1811.

Road Bridges

Three road bridges across the Danube link the Slovak left bank with the Hungarian right bank. At km 1806, the road leads 12 km south to the old bishopric of Györ, formerly Raab under the Austro-Hungarian Empire. With its break-up, the towns of **Komárno** on the Slovak side and **Komárom** on the Hungarian side (km 1768) were created in 1920. Massive fortifications on both sides of the river recall the fear of Turkish attacks in the 16th and 17th century and remain the chief sights to be seen in both towns.

The **Maria-Valeria Bridge** between Stúrovo and Esztergom (km 1719) is an expression of the new European *rapprochement*. It was first built in 1895. After its destruction by German troops in World War II (1944), a firm link between the Slovak and Hungarian towns was re-established only in 2001.

Esztergom

Some 150 km (93 miles) southeast of Bratislava, Esztergom (km 1718), was Hungary's first capital and royal seat under the Árpád kings. King Stephen was born

here around 970, and founded the cathedral in 1010. The monarchy moved out after the Mongol invasions of the 13th century, but the archbishops stayed on, taking over the royal residence. Esztergom was to pay for its ecclesiastical importance in 1543, when it was destroyed by the Turks. The restoration needed was so extensive that the Church only moved back again in 1820. And despite its clergy facing brutal persecution by the Communist authorities in the 1950s and 60s, the city has remained the centre of Hungarian Catholicism.

Basilica

The gigantic neoclassical basilica that towers over the city skyline is on the site of King Stephen's original cathedral. Begun in 1822, it took nearly 40 years to complete. The dome is based on St Peter's in Rome.

The most outstanding feature of the voluminous interior is the Bakócz Chapel, built in red marble by Florentine Renaissance craftsmen in the early 16th century. It's the only part of the old cathedral left.

To the right of the main altar, the treasury contains a magnificent collection of textiles and medieval gold relics, including the 13th-century Coronation Cross used by Hungary's kings to pledge their oaths up to the last coronation—Karl IV—in 1916. In the crypt is the tomb of Cardinal József Mindszenty. He opposed the Communist takeover after the war and was arrested and tortured. Released during the 1956 Uprising, he took refuge in the US Embassy for the next 15

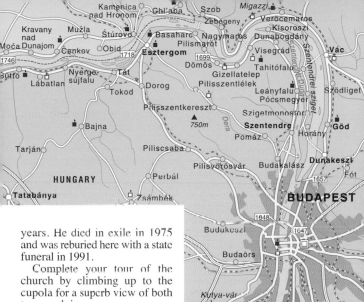

years. He died in exile in 1975 and was reburied here with a state funeral in 1991.

Complete your tour of the church by climbing up to the cupola for a superb view of both town and river.

The **Castle Museum** incorporates parts of the royal palace, including a 12th-century chapel and medieval Hall of Virtues, named after its frescoes.

Vizivaros

Below the hill are the attractive baroque streets of the Vizivaros, or Watertown. The **Parish Church** dates from 1738 and is in Italianate baroque style. In the old Primate's Palace, the **Christian Museum** houses what ranks as Hungary's greatest collection of religious art, with Italian prints, Renaissance paintings and the ornate 15th-century Garamszent-benedek coffin.

Beyond Esztergom

Just beyond Esztergom, the Danube forces its way between mountainsides soaring 300 and 400 m high, in places over 900 m, of the volcanic Börzsöny mountains in the north and the Visegràd range in the south, a stretch of river with glorious views over wooded hills and centuries-old little towns and castles. From km 1708, at the Danube's confluence on the left bank with the Slovak-Hungarian frontier river Ipoly, is the splendid landscape that is part of the **Duna-Ipoly National Park**. With luck, you may even spot the rare Saker falcon or Short-toed snake-eagle *(Circaetus gallicus)*, which breed in these parts.

Danube Bend

At the Danube Bend (around km 1690) the river makes a right-angle turn, from heading roughly, to almost due south. Wooded hills on either side give way here and there to pretty towns and villages dotted along the river banks. They provide an idyllic setting for the remains of King Matthias Corvinus's opulent 15th-century palace at **Visegrad** (km 1695). Much of the sprawling residence —terraced into five levels on the hillside—has been restored. The monumental Hercules Fountain is a fine example of Hungarian Renaissance; the Court of Honour has graceful arcades.

Vác

Vác (km 1680) has a pretty baroque centre, its houses still painted green, red and ochre, compensating for the textile factories and cement works on the outskirts. The 18th-century cathedral boasts remarkable frescoes by Franz Anton Maulpertsch, while the Triumphal Arch (1764) was built specially for a visit by Queen Maria Theresa.

Szentendre

Szentendre (km 1667) is a photogenic little town with a surprising number of art galleries and museums. Founded by Serbian refugees fleeing the Turks after the Battle of Kosovo in 1389, it received a second wave of Serbs three centuries later when the Turks recaptured Belgrade.

The main town square is the baroque Fő tér, with a votive cross put up by Serbian merchants in 1763 to celebrate the non-appearance of the plague. Here, too, is the green-spired Serbian Orthodox Blagoveštenska Church, built ten years earlier. The icons inside are emphatically Serbian, and evoke the troubled history of that land.

Just behind the square's east side, an alley leads to the **Margit**

Taking the Waters. You can't have everything. Hungary, occupying only one per cent of the area of Europe, lacks two significant geographical features: mountains to inspire skiers, and a seacoast. The landlocked country has to make do with the Danube and central Europe's biggest lake, Balaton. Bathing in Lake Balaton, which is rich in calcium and magnesium, is said to be good for you. The water is pleasantly warm, and your feet sink into the soft, sandy bottom, raising clouds of sand. It's certainly good for the fish: some of the pike-perch grow to 10 kg.

Any Hungarians not swimming in the Danube or Balaton are probably immersed in thermal baths. There are about 500 hot springs around the country, much appreciated since the time of the ancient Romans. Soaking in the spa waters—or drinking them—is supposed to cure just about any ailment you can imagine.

VISA/Louvet

Kovács Museum, Vastagh György 1, newly renovated and expanded. Kovács, who died in 1977, created stylized, elongated sculptures, and her work—part reinvention of religious iconic art, part folksy kitsch—is both striking and entertaining.

Skanzen
An open-air museum, 3 km northwest of Szentendre, comprises a collection of typical Hungarian houses and a wooden church of the 18th century.

Szentendre Island
Beyond Visegrád, the Danube forms the 31-km long Szentendre Island, a popular excursion-spot that continues as far as Budapest. Big ships sail along its east side. There on the left bank, they pass by Budapest's first suburbs.

Göd
The church at Göd (km 1663) is a fine example of the so-called organic architecture of its best-known Hungarian exponent, Imre Makovecs.

Budapest
The Hungarian capital Budapest (km 1648), with over 1.6 million inhabitants, conjures up a string of flattering adjectives: dramatic, enchanting, glamorous, magical. It's difficult to decide from which angle the "Paris of the East" is

AUKCIÓSHÁZ

SWAROVSKI

FÉLEMELET

POLGÁR
GALÉRIA

When you go shopping in Budapest's Váci
utca, don't forget to look up at the splendid
architecture.

most breathtaking: looking over the majestic river towards the monumental flat expanses of Pest from the heights of Buda, or rather in the direction of the hills and towers of Buda from Pest down below.

The Castle District

This fascinating zone of cobbled streets, hidden gardens and medieval courtyards hovers over the rest of Budapest on a long, narrow plateau. Towering gracefully above the old town is the neo-Gothic spire of the **Matthias Church**, founded in the 13th century by King Béla IV. The building itself is essentially 19th-century neo-Gothic, attached to what the Turks left of the original edifice in 1686. The Loreto Chapel contains the revered statue of the Virgin once buried by the Turks in the chapel walls. It is said to have reappeared miraculously during the siege of 1686.

Nearby rises an undulating white rampart with gargoyles and cloisters: the **Fishermen's Bastion**. Built on the site of a medieval fish market, it recalls the fact that in the 18th century local fishermen were responsible for defending the fortifications. The present Disneyesque structure dates from early in the 20th century. The arches frame the river artistically, as if they had been designed especially for photographers.

The Royal Palace

After a long and turbulent history, including complete destruction at the end of World War II, the palace begun in the 13th century by Béla IV has been restored to its former splendour and offers a fine view over Pest and the Danube from its walls. The building houses two excellent museums. In the baroque south wing, the **Budapest History Museum** tracks the city's evolution since the Bronze Age. Downstairs in the excavated part of the medieval castle you can see the Gothic Royal Chapel of Matthias I and the Knights' Hall. On the ground floor is a roomful of striking Gothic statues unearthed in 1974. The upper levels house collections covering prehistoric times to the arrival of the Avars. The **Hungarian National Gallery** displays an impressive modern exhibition of Hungarian art from the Middle Ages to the present day. You enter from the terrace overlooking the Danube. Among the most remarkable works, look for the splendid Late Gothic altars, so delicately carved they look like lace.

Danube Views

Gellért Hill takes its name from an Italian missionary (Gerard) who converted the Hungarians but was eventually thrown from the hill in a barrel spiked with nails, in 1046, by militant heathens. His statue stands on the north side of the hill, overlooking the Elizabeth Bridge. At the top of the hill, the severe-looking **Citadel** was built by the Austrians after the 1848 revolution. It served in World War II as the last stronghold of the German occupying army. Their bunker has been converted into the **Panoptikum** wax museum, illustrating the occupation of Budapest in 1944–45. A conspicuous modern addition to the hilltop is the **Liberation Monument**, visible from many parts of the city.

Down below, riverside Buda is known as Watertown because of its thermal baths. **Rudas Gyógyfürdő**, one of the most colourful, has been in business since 1556.

At the Buda side of the 1849 Chain Bridge, a **funicular** reaches Castle Hill just north of the Royal Palace gates. It provides one of the most scenic rides in Budapest, and has been in operation since 1870, when it was driven by steam. It was modernized and electrified in 1986.

A short walk north of the Chain Bridge in Batthyány tér, the twin-towered **St Anne's Church** is one of the most striking baroque structures in the city. Designed by a Jesuit, Ignatius Pretelli, in Italian style in the mid-18th century, the interior is a dazzling drama of huge statues and black marble columns.

The 16th-century Turkish **Király Gyógyfürdő**, with their octagonal pool, are sheltered beneath a stone dome.

Left Bank

To the northwest along the embankment, the neo-Gothic **Houses of Parliament**, looking much like their British counterpart, were built between 1896 and 1902 to symbolize the autonomy of Hungary within the greater grandeur of the Austro-Hungarian Empire. You can take a guided tour and see, among other splendours, the royal sceptre, crown and orb.

Modern luxury hotels dot the river bank as far as the Elizabeth Bridge, which sends traffic hurtling into the centre of historic Pest. The nine Danube bridges in Budapest are completed by Liberty and Petőfi bridges. South of this last stands the modern **Palace of Arts,** opened in 2005 and venue of high-class concerts, as well as the **Ludwig Museum** displaying contemporary art with works by Picasso, Baselitz, Lichtenstein alongside Hungarian artists like Endre Tót, Molnár and Erdély.

Pest

The oldest surviving structure in Pest, nestled against the flyover leading to Elizabeth Bridge, is the **Inner City Parish Church**. Founded in the 12th century, it served the Turks as a mosque.

The cobbled centrepiece of an expansive pedestrian zone, **Váci utca** is packed with shops selling wine and food, art and antiques, cosmetics, fashion and jewellery. Street vendors hawk all manner of goods. There are several cafés and restaurants where you can sit back and contemplate the street's eclectic architectural mix.

Vestiges of the city's medieval walls have been attractively incorporated into more recent buildings, notably in the streets that form part of the **Kiskörút** boulevard, bending its way from the Szabadság Bridge to Deák tér, and changing names along the way. One of its most fascinating landmarks is at 1 Vámház körút, a cavernous red-brick and cast-iron **covered market**, full of local colour and exotic smells. It opened in 1897.

The Múzeum körút section is dominated by the **Hungarian National Museum**, with a magnificent neoclassical façade. The huge exhibition covers the entire drama of the nation's history from the Stone Age to the collapse of communism. The oldest collections are on the ground floor, including extraordinary jewellery of gold and precious stones.

Matthias Church in Buda, with its colourful tiled roof. | A quick way up to the Royal Palace.

BUDAVÁRI SIKLÓ

Vámház körút and Múzeum körút intersect at Kálvin tér, where you might wish to make a foray into Üllöi út to visit the extraordinary building housing the **Museum of Applied Arts**. The style of this brick-and-ceramic-tile palace is listed as Art Nouveau, though it might be better described as Fantasy Hungarian with strong eastern influences.

Further south, on Páva útca, the **Holocaust Museum** was inaugurated in 2004. It includes a long-abandoned synagogue that has been magnificently renovated, as well as a new building complex. The synagogue is open to the public. The museum has permanent and temporary exhibitions.

Andrássy út, 2.5 km long, was modelled in the 19th century after the Champs-Elysées. The neo-Renaissance **State Opera House** is the most admired building on the avenue, which ends with a flourish at **Heroes' Square**, with the Millenary Monument as its centrepiece, topped by a statue of the Archangel Gabriel. Facing each other across the Square are two neoclassical buildings. The larger one is the **Museum of Fine Arts**, whose comprehensive collection of paintings, including a number of French Impressionists, gives it an international importance. The smaller Art Gallery holds temporary exhibitions of paintings by Hungarian and foreign artists.

Among the amenities of the **City Park** is the Castle of Vajdahunyad, modelled on a Transylvanian castle. It houses the Hungarian Museum of Agriculture. Outside is a hooded figure representing the 12th-century chronicler Anonymus. You'll notice the triple dome of the **Széchenyi Baths**, one of Europe's largest spa complexes. The sight of people playing chess while soaking in the healing waters is not to be missed.

South of Budapest

On this stretch, the Danube is bordered by dense shrubbery and trees, on the right for the first 100 km south of Budapest most often a tall river bank on which villages are more frequently seen than in the flat country on the left bank.

Dunaúváros

The steel centre of Dunaújváros (km 1578), designed after World War II, was built with its large harbour on the site of the Roman military base of Intercisum. The industrial town has a garden of archaeological ruins and a museum devoted to the Roman fortifications.

Dunaföldvár

Dunaföldvár (km 1560), where a bridge spans the Danube, recalls the era of Turkish invasions with its Turkish bastion and the castle museum.

Harta

Harta (km 1546) on the left bank dates back to Swabian (German) settlers brought here by Austria's Archduchess Maria Theresa in the 18th century.

Paks

The major attractions here are the Church of the Holy Ghost designed by Imre Makovecs and the renowned fish-soup of Paks (km 1531), as well as the country's only nuclear power station south of town (km 1526).

Kalocsa

The farming town of Kalocsa (km 1516) has something for every taste—history, folklore, art, and one of Europe's most offbeat museums. Kalocsa was founded in the 11th century alongside the Danube, but the river subsequently changed its mood and its course, leaving the town 6 km from the nearest fish or boat. Happily, the newly enlarged boundaries of Kalocsa included fertile meadows, where fruit and vegetables and grain grow. The dominant crop, though, is red paprika. So it is that Kalocsa offers the **Paprika Museum**, where you can follow the saga of the Mexican hot pepper through its Hungarian naturalization. It did not become an essential ingredient of the Hungar-

The Puszta. Also known as the Great Plain (Nagy Alföld), the vast, flat prairie of the Puszta was Hungary's very own Wild West during the 19th century, when huge herds of cattle grazed here watched over by cowboys, called gulyás. It was once covered in thick forest, but was laid waste during the Turkish occupation, because of the invaders' need for timber to build fortresses, and became a virtual desert. Its renaissance as pastureland was due to the irrigation works on the River Tisza employed by Count Széchenyi in the early 19th century. But by the 20th century, the success of the irrigation scheme meant it could sustain crop development, and big landowners carried out wholesale enclosure, killing off the cattle industry and creating widespread poverty among the peasants. Under post-war communism, the estates were nationalized, and huge collective farms introduced, only to be broken up after 1989 and returned to private ownership. Today, you will find pleasant little towns—Kecskemét and Szeged in particular are worth spending time in—beyond which are attractive old whitewashed farmsteads adorned with bright-coloured strings of paprika.

istockphoto.com/Ferenc

A fleeting encounter in the Kiskunság National Park.

ian diet until the early 19th century. One of the town's most photogenic features is the display, every autumn, of bright red peppers hanging to dry from the eaves of local houses.

Main Square

Kalocsa's main square, Szabadság tér, features statues of two national heroes—King (Saint) Stephen and Franz (Ferenc in Hungarian) Liszt. The 18th-century cathedral, in graceful baroque style, stands on the site of a series of churches, going back to the

11th century. In the **Archbishop's Palace** across the square, the library contains over 100,000 volumes, including a Bible autographed by Martin Luther.

Károly Viski Museum

In Kalocsa there's no shortage of folklore exhibits. The peasant costumes are a delight of floral designs. Here, too, are displays of traditional farm tools, antique furniture and decorations.

Schoeffer Museum

A master of kinetic art, Nicolas Schoeffer (1912–92) donated some of his works to his home town; they are displayed in his house of birth, at Szent István Király út 76, the same street as the Viski Museum.

Museum of Folk Art

Run by the Kalocsa Folk Art Co-operative, the museum displays antique agricultural implements and rustic furnishings. Kalocsa embroidery is on show—and on sale—and they stage folklore exhibitions in which the local youngsters dance to typically vivacious Hungarian music.

Puszta

The Hungarian version of the wild west conjures visions of gallant horsemen, lonely shepherds, pastures and dunes. It's all still there in Kiskunság National Park,

35,000 protected hectares (86,000 acres) of dramatic landscape between the Danube and the Tisza. Accomplished horsemen in baggy trousers and red waistcoats show the tourists their skills in a cross between a rodeo and a circus. Apart from the handsome horses there are herds of big-horned cattle and Racka sheep with screw-shaped horns.

One of the highlights of a visit to the puszta is a stop at a *czárda*, or wayside inn, where the food is as rustic as the surroundings. The meal is washed down with hearty Hungarian wine and the wail of gypsy violins, or the spirited melodies of the czárdás.

Kiskunság National Park

In the sandy highlands between the Danube and the Tisza, the park (760 sq km) comprising nine separate areas, preserves for posterity the historical landscapes of the Puszta and important nature reserves. Most of them have been declared UNESCO Biosphere Reserves. You will come across the region's typical domestic and pasturing animals as well as rare bird species such as spoonbills, purple herons and silver herons.

Sió Valley

Just beyond a modern motorway bridge (km 1499) spanning the now slowly flowing Danube, surrounded mostly by lush marshy

woodland is the confluence with the River Sió, transformed here into a canal for its 123-km course from Lake Balaton, plied by pleasure boats and ships.

Szekszárd

Above the Sió Valley, about 15 km west of the Danube, Szekszárd is the centre of a wine-growing region. The county seat, it has a high proportion of citizens of German and Serbian descent. Their pedigree can be traced back to the 150 years of Turkish occupation, when Szekszárd was a ghost town. To renew the population in the 18th century, settlers from neighbouring countries were welcomed. Local history starts in the 11th century, when King Béla I founded a fortified Benedictine monastery on a hill. The courtyard of the present County Hall is built around the remains of an ancient chapel and the abbey church.

Baja

Along a stretch of the Danube surrounded by virgin forests as far as Baja (km 1479), you reach the southernmost Hungarian bridge on the Danube. Over this vital link between east and west Hungary carries rail traffic as well as cars and trucks (eastbound and westbound alternate), all on a single lane. Long before there was a bridge, the Turkish invaders, aware of the strategic significance, fortified the town. Today the enormous main square, Béke tér, gives an idea of the historic importance of Baja.

Duna-Drava National Park

From the lower reaches of the Sió in the north to Hungary's southern border, the park covers a surface of 500 sq km through which the Danube flows for 65 km as well as a portion of its Drava tributary. Across the sometimes narrow, sometimes several kilometres wide floodplain with often impenetrable forest, countless tributary streams, dead arms of the river and stagnant pools form a landscape constantly changing with the considerable seasonal variations in water levels. Danube travellers make their way for hours through this wild landscape of water, woods and islands along the meandering branches of the main river. White egrets and grey herons, cormorants and wild ducks throng the banks, osprey and black stork breed on the reserve.

Gemenc Forest

Nature lovers can explore this northwest area of the national park along nature trails via a narrow-gauge railway and on boat tours. Besides rare birds, they may also spot deer, stag, beaver and wild boar.

Mohács

The Danube port city of Mohács (km 1447) is forever linked with a melancholy chapter in Hungarian history. It unfolded swiftly, a few kilometres out of town, on August 29, 1526. A well-equipped army of Sultan Suleiman the Magnificent, with a four-to-one advantage in manpower, crushed the defending forces of the Hungarian King Louis (Lajos) II. The king died during the retreat. For the next century and a half Hungary endured Ottoman occupation.

The modern **Votive Church** in the centre of town is one of the local memorials to these events. Meant to give thanks for the eventual expulsion of the Turks, it might be mistaken for a mosque, but for the dome topped by a big cross.

On the actual site of the battle, a **Memorial Park** is strewn with haunting modern sculptures symbolizing the opposing forces. The ghosts of the generals, the soldiers and the horses—in imaginative wood-carvings—are forever deployed across the field of battle. The park was dedicated in 1976 on the 450th anniversary of an unforgettable defeat.

The people of Mohács celebrate the departure of the Turks at Carnival time, when they parade in the scariest giant masks. The Busó carnival also aims to expel another invader—winter.

PÉCS

On the southern slopes of the Mecsek hills, west of Mohács, 200 km south of Budapest, the university town of Pécs (population 155,000) is the largest city in Transdanubia. Chosen as European Capital of Culture in 2010, the city is being rejuvenated, and the historic core carefully restored. On the ancient trade route from the German-speaking countries to the Balkans and Middle East, Pécs unites cultures of east, west and south.

You will see traces left behind by the former inhabitants, Celts, Romans, Turks, Germans and Hungarians. In Roman times, Hadrian called the town Sopianae and made it the capital of Pannonia. Some parts of the **Roman aqueduct** can still be seen, and many fine relics of prehistoric and Roman times are displayed in the **Janus Pannonius Museum**.

The Hungarians conquered the area in the late 9th century and their king Stephen (István, 997–1038) made Pécs an ecclesiastical centre. The first **cathedral** burnt down in 1064, but it was replaced in the 11th century by the building you see today at the top of Dóm tér. Each of its four corners are topped by a tower.

The crypt, with its five naves, is the oldest part of the building; the cathedral was re-worked in the 19th century in the Tuscan Romanesque style, seen in the eleven arches of the south façade. In Roman times, the square was the centre of a cemetery and many early Christian burial vaults have been excavated. This **necropolis** is a UNESCO World Heritage Site and opened to the public in 2007.

King Matthias built the circular, crenellated **Barbacan**, a gate tower for the castle. It stands next to the Bishops' Palace. After the Battle of Mohács in 1526, the Ottoman army invaded Pécs. The city was occupied by the Turks from 1543. Churches were turned into mosques, Turkish baths and minarets were built, and a bazaar replaced the market. The Turks also introduced new kinds of grapes, among them *kadarka*.

After the expulsion of the Turks, Pécs became part of the Habsburg Empire. The large main mosque, built in honour of Pasha Kasim, has been transformed into the parish church. It stands at the top of Széchenyi tér. The high round dome and striped arches remain from the Muslim era, but the congregation is now

Hungarian and Catholic, and a crucifix stands over the prayer niche. A marble tablet inscribed in elegant Arabic calligraphy spells out a verse of the Koran translated into Hungarian.

On Rákóczi út, another mosque, **Pasha Hassan Yakovali** is still a place of Muslim worship and a small museum displaying Turkish armour, stirrups, rugs, pottery and utensils; it is the only mosque in Hungary whose minaret is intact.

From the early 18th century, under the Habsburgs, the city flourished. Queen Maria Theresa granted Pécs the status of a free royal town. The architecture of many grand residences and public bulding in ornate baroque style dates back to this period.

Industry continued to develop in the second half of the 19th century: iron foundries, paper-makers, sugar-refineries and coal-mining were significant, and the **Zsolnay Porcelain** works were established in 1853. Zsolnay majolica adorns many of the town house façades. The 1869 **Synagogue**, on Goldmark Károly utca, bears a plaque honouring the local victims of Auschwitz—88 per cent of the city's Jews perished in World War II.

By the early 20th century, Pécs had developed to become one of Hungary's biggest towns. Its citi-

David Warden

The porcelain bull's heads decorating the Zsolnay Fountain have a metallic sheen.

zens built Eclectic-style houses, a splendid National Theatre on Kossuth Lajos utca, a fine Town Hall, coffee houses, and an ornate railway station. The only Art Nouveau building in the city, the main **Post Office** on Jókai utca bears witness to this period.

One of Péc's famous sons was Victor Vasarely (1906–1997); the father of Op-Art donated many of his works to the city; they are displayed in the **Vasarely Museum** on Káptalan utca. Opposite is the Decorative Arts section of the Janus Pannonius Museum, with Zsolnay ceramics.

A skein of birds flies over the reserve of Kopački Rit, between Danube and Drava.

Kroatische Zentrale für Tourismus

Downriver to Belgrade

After leaving Hungary at km 1433, the Danube serves for about 137 km (85 miles) as a frontier (still disputed) between Croatia and Serbia, and is no longer called Duna, but Dunav.

Bezdan

A bridge (km 1425) links the hillside Croatian village of Batina with the little Serbian town of Bezdan, 5 km away. This is the western end of the canal network started in the early 19th century and frequently expanded—between the Danube and Tisza. The historic locks designed by Gustave Eiffel in 1880 on the 123-km **Veliki-Bački Canal** to the Tisza is, like many other sections of the artificial network of waterways, no longer practicable for modern commercial shipping.

Apatin

The **Banat**, a fertile plain bounded by the Danube and Tisza, was settled by Swabians from Germany after the Turks were driven out. Incidentally, many of the immigrants found jobs on Danube ships.

German settlers also founded Apatin (km 1401) in the 18th century. The town became famous for its hemp ropes and beer and even today the view over the Serbian town is dominated by the gigantic silos of the Jelen brewery. But now only a small proportion of the population is German-speaking.

Kopački Rit

The extensive floodplain landscape of the River Drava's confluence region is very much in evidence right here on the Croatian bank. The river has its source in the Alps and raises its water level considerably after the snow thaw and autumn rains. The Kopački Rit nature reserve located in the wedge of land between the Danube and Drava is a 177 sq-km Eldorado for fish and one of the most important bird sanctuaries in Europe. Tens of thousands of migratory birds spend their winter here, among them the rare greater spotted eagle, while the black stork and white-tailed sea eagle rear their young here. The Danube winds its way as far as the mouth of the Drava (km 1383) and beyond in many curves with greatly increased water volume. Islands, lateral branches of the river and shallows complicate the ships' passage.

Osijek

The most important town in the region of Slavonia at the eastern edge of Croatia, Osijek lies 20 km upstream on the Drava and

Croatian National Tourist Board

The red rooftops of the pretty baroque city of Osijek by the Drava.

dral of Peter and Paul (1898). The man who initiated its construction was Bishop Josip Jurak Strossmayer (1819–1905), born in Osijek and politically very active for the Croatian cause from his diocese in Đakovo.

Đakovo

In this little town some 60 km to the south, the outstanding monument is the huge neo-Romanesque and neo-Gothic cathedral of St Peter, built 1888–82 and Strossmayer's burial place. This rustic centre is known for its annual embroidery folklore festival in July and for its 500-year-old stud farm. For 200 years it has specialized in the breeding of Lipizzaners (stars of Vienna's Spanish Riding School), trained here as coach-horses.

has over 90,000 inhabitants. In the course of history, Illyrians, Romans, Hungarians and Slavs lived here by the river. The Turks built a wooden bridge over the Drava with a fortress which the Habsburgs later transformed into a baroque stronghold (Croatian Tvrđa). Town life, brightened up by its university students, focuses today further upstream on Europska Avenija, which is lined with ornate historical buildings in Art Nouveau and Vienna Secession style. On the skyline looms the tower of the neo-Gothic co-cathe-

Vukovar

The port of Vukovar (km 1333) serves as a gateway for excursions into Croatia's fertile rural region west of the Danube. Visible from the river, the bullet-riddled water tower makes a sad landmark, The capital of the Srijem region, with its churches, patrician houses and arcaded passages near the baroque castle of the counts of Eltz, was once regarded as a jewel of urban baroque architecture. In 1991, it fell victim to the civil war in former Yugoslavia. After Serbian-occupied eastern Slavonia was restored to Croatia in 1998, reconstruction began in earnest. Restored historical edifices as well as modern buildings now offer hope for a renaissance of the most important Croatian port town on the Danube.

Ilok

The Srijem landscape, where Romans introduced vineyards, extends past the little Croatian town of Ilok (km 1299). The hill close to the river bank makes an ideal lookout, site of the medieval fortification protected by a town wall of bricks. The restored church tower of the Franciscan monastery juts out as a last bastion of predominantly Catholic Croatia. Across the Danube and just a few kilometres away in the hinterland is the mainly Orthodox Serbia.

Bačka Palanka

A bridge (km 1297) links Ilok with the Serbian town of Bačka Palanka, an important agricultural centre. From km 1296, the Danube flows for 221 km through Serbia.

Fruška Gora

In the hinterland behind the right bank are the wooded hills of Fruška Gora, over 500 m high, with grapes and plums growing on the slopes.

Far away in the hills, 16 Orthodox monasteries lie hidden, mostly built in the 16th century. A national park covering 250 sq km protects the nature and culture of these hills.

Rain Dance. The Indians of North America are not the only ones who perform dances to pray for rain: similar customs have also been known on the Danube. In Serbia's Bačka Palanka, men and women would dance at the harvest festival, douse each other with water and sing for the heavens to open. A group of girls would proceed through the village, their leader clad only in flowers, grass and leaves, to be greeted from each threshold with a bucketful of water.

Novi Sad

At km 1255, this is the principal town of **Vojvodina**, the granary of former Yugoslavia. Founded at the end of the 17th century by Serbs fleeing from the Turks, Novi Sad was declared a royal free city in 1748. A century later the Hungarians virtually razed it to the ground. In the 19th century the town was a cultural and intellectual focus for the Serbs within the Austro-Hungarian empire, when it became known as (yet another) Athens of the North.

Architecturally, Novi Sad offers little of interest, but it does have a pleasant museum and an art gallery with an extensive collection of paintings.

In 1999 the three bridges of Novi Sad were destroyed by NATO bombs; since then they have all been replaced; the last, the Sloboda (Liberty) Bridge, was completed in 2005.

Petrovaradin

Standing opposite the town on the right bank of the river, the fortress of Petrovaradin is well worth a visit—take a look at the clock tower: the hour hand is longer than the minute hand. Fortified by monks in the 13th century, the citadel fell to Suleiman the Magnificent three centuries later. Prince Eugène of Savoy—celebrated in folk songs as the "noble knight"—managed to drive out the Turks in 1716. The Austrians undertook construction of a new citadel, using plans drawn up by the famous French military architect Vauban. As Napoleon's armies advanced upon Vienna, the treasures of the Imperial Court were hurried to the safety of

Orthodox saints in the monastery of Novo Hopovo, Fruška Gora. | Fountain in Sremski Karlovci. | Petrovaradin fortress. | The spires of Sremski Karlovci, an attractive baroque city.

THE TISZA

Originating in the Carpathian mountains of western Ukraine, the Tisza winds slowly through Hungary southwards and links up with the Danube in Serbia, just north of Belgrade. It actually flows longer inside Hungary than the Danube. Notorious for flooding, it has been improved by the construction of thousands of kilometres of embankments, straightened out in places and harnessed to provide hydro-electric power and irrigation. The best-known cities along its shores are Tokaj, in the northeast region of Hungary, and Szeged in the south. Tokaj is known for its fine wines and Szeged for spicy salami and a highly seasoned fish soup.

Tokaj lies at the spot where the Tisza makes a 90° turn southwards, at a conjunction with the scenic Bodrog river. Terraced vineyards cling to the hillside above town; the streets are full of wine cellars where you can taste many varieties of their sweet wines. One has been converted into a museum *(Tokaji múzeum)* documenting the ancient methods of production.

Szeged is a river port and cultural centre, boasting two universities which confer on the city a young and cheerful atmosphere. The layout of concentric boulevards and streets on a grid pattern was devised after a devastating flood in 1879. In the town centre on Széchenyi tér, among lawns, flower gardens and fountains, the ornate City Hall, in what is known as Eclectic baroque style, was built after the flood, each floor with its own style of window. South from here is the main shopping area, reserved for pedestrians. The great pinnacled Votive Church *(Fogadalmi templom)*, with eight clocks on its twin towers, was erected as a memorial after the flood, with construction beginning in 1913. The Szeged Summer Festival of opera and ballet is held in the square outside. Nearby is the medieval Tower of St Demetrius, sturdy enough to have resisted destruction. An 18th-century Serbian church boasts a superb collection of Orthodox icons.

By the river at the Palace of Education and Culture, the Ferenc Morá Museum gives insight into Szeged's history, the importance of the River Tisza and has reproductions of peasants' living quarters, Hun and Avar handicrafts.

Petrovaradin. In the mid-19th century, Hungarian freedom fighters captured the fortress, but they were overcome by loyalist Croats and Serbs. For a long time afterwards the citadel served as both barracks and prison, housing such illustrious inmates as Josip Broz, later to become Marshal Tito.

Sremski Karlovci

Continuing downriver you reach Sremski Karlovci (km 1246), a pretty little town with fine baroque houses. It's famous in history as the place where the peace treaty of 1699 (the Treaty of Karlowitz) was signed by Austria, Turkey, Poland and Venice, putting an end to the war with the Turks and giving Austria supremacy in the Balkans. Apparently the room in which the treaty was signed had to be provided

with four doors, as the delegations couldn't come to an agreement as to which of them was to enter first.

To return to the present, Sremski Karlovci is also known for its excellent red wine (and also its rosé); the best place to sample them is right here on the spot.

Stari Slankamen

The stronghold of Stari Slankamen (km 1215) is a reminder of a battle against the Ottomans in 1691; today's visitors come for a peaceful soak in the warm, sodium-rich waters of the geothermal springs.

Zemun

Zemun (km 1173), now just a suburb of Belgrade, was founded by the Romans, who called it Taurunum. After 1526 the Turks

fortified the town; later it fell to Austria, and until 1918 the Hungarian border ran past here.

Belgrade

The capital of Serbia, Belgrade (Beograd; km 1170) is one of four capital cities standing on the Danube. Along with Vienna, Bratislava and Budapest, it was a crucial site in Europe's commercial and communications network even before Roman times.

When the Roman Empire was split into East and West in 395, the seat of power moved from Rome to Constantinople. Byzantium was allotted Belgrade in its portion, and the boundary between the two parts of the empire ran beneath the city walls. The division is still mirrored in Belgrade's adherence to the Orthodox faith, which evolved throughout Byzantium. The Byzantines were not alone in coveting Belgrade. Bulgars, Hungarians, Austrians and Turks all held it over the ages. The Turks left only in 1867, and if you keep your eyes open, you will sense the Orient's former sway.

The city was badly bombed in the two world wars of the 20th century, and because of its strategic situation, was occupied by Austria and Germany. Belgrade has been destroyed and rebuilt 20 times, so apart from the ancient fortress that has known so many masters, little is really old.

The postwar period has seen it change from a small Balkan town to a modern European metropolis, with a population of more than a million, and capital of Serbia. In rebuilding, the emphasis was placed on the scientific, edu-

cational, cultural and conference infrastructures. The country has officially applied for membership of the EU, setting its goal for 2014.

Fortress

Looming over the meeting point of the Danube and the Sava is the old fortress within three sets of ramparts, watching over its upper and lower towns. The Romans built their fortifications up on the hill in the 1st century, and they were reinforced by the Byzantines several centuries later. When the Austrians occupied the fortress in 1717–39, after temporarily dislodging the Turks, they made it one of the mightiest bastions of all Europe. Today the citadel houses a military museum, and everything speaks of the passage of time. Within the upper walls are some ancient remains: a Roman well, a Turkish mausoleum, a corbelled building used by the cultural authorities of the city, and a statue of the Victor of Belgrade, a young soldier carrying a message of peace. The Turkish hammam at the foot of the hill has been converted into a

The sturdy old fortress of Belgrade commands respect. | Folk singers in traditional Serbian costume. | A wide and elegant stairway leads up to Kalemegdan, around the fortress.

planetarium. Kalemegdan, the area around the fortress, is now a pleasant park with a zoo, children's amusement park, sports grounds and restaurants.

Old Town

Danube ships anchor on the Sava, a short walk from the fortress and old town. Just outside the fortress is the old quarter of Varoš kapija (City Gate), where you'll find several interesting buildings. The Patriarch's residence houses the **Museum of the Serbian Orthodox Church**. Opposite is the **cathedral** (*Saborna crkva*), built in neoclassical style in 1837–40. Several religious figures and Serbian overlords are buried beneath the altar and in the crypt, among them Prince Miloš Obrenović, one of the leaders of the second Serbian revolt against the Turks, who set a dynasty on the throne (1815–42 then 1858–1903). The same prince had a pretty white mansion, the **Residence of Princess Ljubica** (*Konak knjeginje Ljubice*) built for his wife in 1831. Full of antique furniture and ornaments, its Turkish baths, oriental carpets and floor-level seating show how the Turks influenced the lifestyle of the Serbian rulers.

Running southeast of the fortress, the old Roman road to the south, **Knez Mihailova Street**, is now a protected pedestrian area. You can stroll past shops and art galleries right through to Terazije Square, looking up to admire the baroque, Art Nouveau and Social Realist façades. At the end of the street is Republic Square, where you'll find the **National Theatre** (*Narodno pozorište*), an equestrian statue of Prince Mihajlo Obrenović, and the **National Museum** (*Narodni muzej*), due to re-open in 2011 after renovation. Its collections include prehistoric weapons and jewellery, icons and religious books, Serbian and European art.

Other Museums

Only the museums safeguard the city's historical memories. Visit the **Ethnographic Museum** (*Etnografski muzej*), devoted to Serbian arts and folklore, and the **Museum of Contemporary Art** (*Muzej savremene umetnosti*) on the other side of the Sava, at Novi Beograd. North of this commercial district is Zemun (see p. 70).

St Sava Cathedral

Looking back over the city, you can't miss its dome, dominating the skyline. Construction began in the early 20th century and was completed in 1995, though it will take years to finish its interior decoration. This is the largest Orthodox church in the world, big enough to hold a congregation of 11,000. Belgrade is in fact a city of many places of worship.

Topčider
Further south stretches Topčider's lovely park, planted with plane trees and a central flowerbed. There are several cafés and the historic palace of Prince Miloš Obrenović, built 1831–33. On the other side of the crossroads is his private chapel, in typical baroque style.

Skadarlija
After exploring the city, you may feel that everything is still haunted by a tragic past. Switch to a lighter mood by spending a few hours in the old bohemian district of Skadarlija—in fact just one sloping cobbled street. Here in the evening, among the numerous small art galleries you'll come across painters selling their canvasses, roving actors, fortune-tellers and musicians, all in a good-humoured atmosphere. The music played in the cosy restaurants and wine houses goes on until the small hours.

Mount Avala
One of the most popular side trips is to Mount Avala, 18 km (11 miles) away, with its Monument to the Unknown Soldier of World War I at the top, the work of Ivan Mešitrović.

Mouth of the Sava
Cruise shops dock on the right bank of the broad Sava river. It's well worth taking the impressive cruise at the mouth of the Sava to see the old fortress and the hill watching over the city.

A road and railway bridge crosses the Danube at km 1167.

From Belgrade to Smederevo
Fed by numerous tributaries on its way to the Black Sea, the Danube below Belgrade swells to a width of almost 1500 m (1640 yd), which makes it Europe's widest river.

It now flows through fertile plains towards the Carpathians. Citadels and fortresses dotted along the banks bear witness to a turbulent history.

Smederevo
The fortress of Smederevo or Semendria (km 1116) was coveted and fought over by various powers. It was built by the Serbian despot Djuradj Branković in 1430, only to be captured by the Ottomans in 1459. The historic fortification was badly damaged by the bombardments of World War II, but still seems to stand in proud defiance of all foes. Branković's cruel wife Jerina, who forced the people of the town to build the fortress despite fearful sacrifices, lives on in Serbian folktales.

Today the ruined wasteland, covering 10 ha, includes a football pitch. After the pipeline bridge (km 1113) to the Smederevska Ada Island, a road bridge (km 1112) is the last solid link across the river for the following 169 km.

On the right bank you will see the mouth of the Morava (km 1104). Further on, on a level with the Kostolac coal-transportation centre (km 1094), the little River Mlava flows into the Danube. The ancient town of Viminacium once stood here; it was the capital of the Roman province of Moesis Superior.

Around Ram

Just before the start of the border with Romania, the small 16th-century fortress of **Ramski Grad** (km 1077) was built by the Turks and later belonged to other overlords.

A ferry links the town of Ram with **Banatska Palanka**, the last Serbian town on the Danube left bank. Shortly afterwards, the winding lower reaches of the River Nera form the border with Romania (km 1075).

For the next 229 km, the Danube serves as the Romanian-Serbian border.

The cool and elegant outline of St Sava Cathedral in Belgrade. | Rustic gathering in the Serbian countryside. | Natural wonders are not very far from the modern centre of Belgrade.

The ruins of Golubac Castle, clinging to its rock.

Downriver to Bucharest

Now the Danube leaves the Pannonian Basin and draws ever closer to the South Carpathian mountains.

Veliko Gradište

The Serbian town of Veliko Gradište (km 1059), where lucrative copper deposits were exploited under the Roman Emperor Hadrian, is now a stopover for international shipping to undergo a border control.

Moldova Veche

Just after Moldova Veche (km 1048), on the site of the Roman settlement of Mudava and once an important station for shipping, the river flows into a narrow defile, 130 km (80 miles) long, separating the Carpathian Mountains from the Balkans. In some places, the sheer rock walls on each side of the river rise to a height of over 700 m (2,300 ft). Once feared for its rapids and cataracts, the terror of sailors in bygone days, the cataract channel was tamed by the construction of a dam and the gigantic Đerdap hydroelectric power station, inaugurated in 1971.

The current is still strong at the narrows, but the water level is today 35 m higher than before the building of the dam's weir. Some 25,000 inhabitants of 17 towns along the former course of the Danube had to be resettled.

To the Iron Gate

The journey through the towering mountain ranges on each side of the river, known in its last part as the Iron Gate, still has the power to impress today's voyagers.

Golubac Castle

On the right bank emerges the gloomy silhouette of Golubac castle (km 1039). Despite its ruined state, the castle, held by the Turks for 260 years, inspires respect with its nine massive towers joined by a ring of walls. Rising steeply from the depths of the river, the Babakai rock has been the inspiration for many myths and legends.

Gorges and Đerdap National Park

The narrow reaches of the river that follow with their steep gorges (Klissura) alternating with bays and wider stretches present not only enchanting landscapes but also historic and prehistoric landmarks. Serbia has created the Đerdap National Park out of a strip of hinterland 2 to 8 km wide along the 103-km stretch of the Danube from the Golubac fortress to the Đerdap 1 power station. The park covers an area of 636 sq km.

Along the **Golubac Klissura** or Gorge (km 1040–km 1026) a

plaque at km 1036 commemorates Gabriel Barosz. As Hungarian minister of transport from 1886 to 1892, he introduced the necessary adjustments for the dangerous Danube rapids.

In the adjoining **Ljubkova Basin** (km 1026–1015) are the villages of Ljubcova, Berzasca and Drencova. The Serbian village of Dobra (km 1021) is built along the narrow wooded valley of a tributary, with its picturesque cemetery located directly on the Danube river bank. **Drencova** (km 1016) was once the last stop for steamships, with passengers disembarking for smaller vessels or taking a coach to circumvent the cataracts.

Upper Klissura is the name of the narrow valley that extends from km 1015 to km 999. At km 1011, a plaque (visible only when the

water level is low enough) recalls the road building under Emperor Tiberius (AD 14–37) and his successors. The Roman road was hewn from the rock or ran for some stretches as a gallery formed by beams set in the rock. It was completed under Trajan (98–117) but now lies submerged beneath the river's higher water level.

Lepenski Vir

The settlement of Lepenski Vir (km 1004) dates back to 8000–4000 BC but was not discovered until 1965. To protect it, archeologists transferred the buildings to higher ground on a hill above the river. The complex ground plans of the excavated buildings testify to a high level of cultural development, and the large river pebbles which were

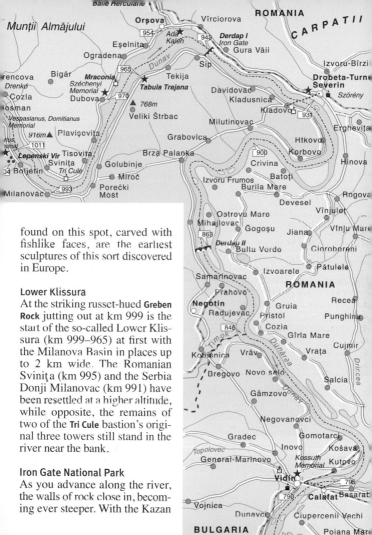

found on this spot, carved with fishlike faces, are the earliest sculptures of this sort discovered in Europe.

Lower Klissura

At the striking russet-hued **Greben Rock** jutting out at km 999 is the start of the so-called Lower Klissura (km 999–965) at first with the Milanova Basin in places up to 2 km wide. The Romanian Sviniţa (km 995) and the Serbia Donji Milanovac (km 991) have been resettled at a higher altitude, while opposite, the remains of two of the **Tri Cule** bastion's original three towers still stand in the river near the bank.

Iron Gate National Park

As you advance along the river, the walls of rock close in, becoming ever steeper. With the Kazan

Narrows (km 974–965) you come to the most spectacular stretch of gorges. Romania named this part of the river bank region Portile de Fier (Iron Gate) National Park.

Ships are obliged to pass singly through the entrance and exit of the **Upper Kazan** (km 974–970), because the navigable channel is scarcely 100 m wide, with a strong current and riverbed over 80 m deep. The roads here on the Serbian and Romanian side often disappear through tunnels or sometimes wind back into the hinterland.

Dubova

At Dubova (km 970), the Danube widens into a bay only to then immediately revert to the picturesque narrows of the **Lower Kazan** (km 969–965), which are enhanced at km 967 on an exposed part of the Romanian bank by a small church.

At the nearby mouth of the little River Mraconia, travellers are watched over by the grim face of Decebalus, last prince of the Dracians (87–106), a 40-m relief sculpted in the rock.

Decebalus glares at the cruise passengers passing by his image. | The Tabula Trajana, Roman history on the Danube. | A fisherman shows off his catch of the day.

Tabula Trajana

On the right bank, look out for the weathered marble Trajan's Plaque (km 965) set here in AD 101 in honour of the Roman emperor. In a few unpretentious words, it commemorates the construction of Trajan's Road along the Danube, a great feat for the time. The plaque was actually moved a little further up the bank from its original position when the reservoir was built.

Orşova

The riverbed widens into the Orşova Basin (km 965–950). Excursion ships dock at the Serbian town of Tekija (km 956). Opposite, the railway and busy European motorway E70 lead down to the deeply indented Bay of Orşova (km 954). The village lies in the greenery on the west side of the bay, crowned by the St Ana convent, while the view on the east side is dictated by the activity of the modern harbour and its wharves.

Unfortunately nothing could be done to save the old town of Orşova, which dated back to the Roman settlement of Tierna, the end point of Trajan's Road. It disappeared beneath the waters when the river was dammed.

Băile Herculane

From Orşova you can make an interesting side-trip to the nearby spa of Băile Herculane (Baths of Hercules) in the narrow Cerna valley, 17 km north of the river. These hot sulphurous springs (over 40 °C) set amidst delightful countryside have lost none of the popularity they used to enjoy in Roman times. In the 19th century the spa resort was frequented by a wealthy clientèle mainly made up of members of the Austro-Hungarian bourgeoisie. Franz-Joseph and his wife each had their own pavilion. People came to cure rheumatism, as well as nervous and digestive problems. In winter, you can ski on nearby slopes.

Ada Kaleh

The island of Ada Kaleh (km 952) suffered the same fate as ancient Orşova and Trajan's Road when the dam was built for the hydroelectric plant at the Iron Gate. A fragment of the Orient in the middle of the Danubian region was lost, its Turkish coffee houses, bazaars, picturesque alleys and gardens, and its characteristic atmosphere submerged for ever beneath the river. Attempts were made to rescue a few buildings on Simian Island further downstream (km 927).

Iron Gate:
Đerdap Power Station

The Iron Gate was opened to large ships after the inauguration of the gigantic Đerdap hydroelec-

In the distance the river narrows at the Iron Gate.

tric power station in 1971, a joint venture between Romania and Serbia. To pass the Iron Gate in the old days, your ship would have been towed by locomotive and tug along a canal to avoid the danger spot. The riverscape has greatly changed, but at least ships can now sail cheerfully through.

At the **Đerdap 1** Locks (km 943), it takes 90 minutes for boats to clear the 34-m lift in the step-locks' two boat tanks, each 310 m long and 30 m wide.

The power station had unexpected consequences for the stur-geon that used to swim upstream from the Black Sea to spawn, providing a rich harvest of caviar for the local fishermen. Now they can not get through the locks.

Drobeta-Turnu Severin

The ancient Dacian settlement of Drobeta-Turnu Severin (km 931) takes you far back from the achievements of the 20th century. Under orders from Emperor Trajan, the architect Apollodorus of Damascus built a bridge across the Danube here in AD 103. With 20 arches, it was one of the longest in the empire; two of its piers have survived to the present day. The bridge was demolished under Hadrian, Trajan's succes-sor, but you can still see it what it looked like whole if you take a trip to Rome and examine the reliefs on Trajan's Column. It shows the level of sophistication the Dacian civilization had attained, such as villages with timber houses and linen clothing with Thracian-style trousers.

Today's Turnu Severin is a major port. In Rose Park, statues commemorate Trajan and his rival, the Dacian king Decebalus. Remains of a medieval fortifica-tion date from the days when the Crusaders set off from here for Asia Minor and the Holy Land. The Municipal Museum provides a fascinating glimpse of the town's history.

Đerdap 2

The widening Danube emerges from the mountains in broad loops and arrives after 80 km at Đerdap 2 (km 863), where at the second of Serbia's and Romania's jointly operated power stations the locks have a hoist of only 10 m to clear.

Walachia

The mouth of the River Timok (km 846) marks the border between Serbia and Bulgaria. The Danube enters the great plain of Walachia, flowing wide and powerful and forming for the next 470 km (290 miles) the frontier between Romania and Bulgaria. Each uses its own version of the name: on the Romanian bank the Dunărea flows past flat lands studded with reed-fringed lakes, whilst the Bulgarian bank of the Dunav is often steep and rocky. As the river used to burst its banks here frequently in former times, noone risked building villages by the water's edge.

Vidin

Almost opposite Calafat (km 795), once a fortified city and now an industrial centre, lies the town of Vidin (km 790), one of the most ancient in Bulgaria. Both Celts and Thracians valued this favourable location on the Danube, and the Romans built the fortress of Bononia here, des-

troyed several times by the Huns and Avars. The town's heyday was in the 14th century when, under the name of Bdin, it was capital of the principality of the same name, but it fell to the Ottomans in 1396. The Turkish feudal lord Osman Pazvantoğlu took it as his own personal fief from 1793 to 1807.

Stretch your legs in the park and long, shady promenade along the Danube. If you visit the town be sure to see the interesting mosque and mausoleum-like library (ca. 1800) of Osman Pazvantoğlu, who had rebelled against the Sultan. The mosque is built in typical oriental style but instead of the crescent moon that normally tops the dome, here it is an arrow-head—eloquent testimony to its builder's insubordination.

The fortress of **Baba Vida**, on the river bank in the north part of the park, dates back to the 10th century and was extended and strengthened in the 14th century. Today it serves as backdrop for theatrical performances.

Belogradchik

From Vidin in the Danube plain, an excursion of just 50 km goes into the wooded foothills of the Balkans to the little hill town of Belogradchik nestling against a grandiose backdrop of russet-hued rocks. Winds and rains have carved the conglomerate of sand-

SOFIA

The long 4-hour approach to Sofia from Nikopol or Vidin adds to the excursion to the Bulgarian capital with its passage through widely varying landscapes from the Danube plain into the dramatic Balkan mountains.

Sofia sits in a broad valley at an altitude of 550 m between the emblematic Vitocha mountain range to the south and the Stara Planina (central Balkans) to the north. The Bulgarians affirm that it is one of Europe's most ancient cities, founded 5,000 years ago. When Bulgarian members of parliament chose it as their national capital in 1879, it numbered only 12,000 inhabitants. Viennese architects came to the aide of the Bulgarians to turn it into a real city. The city has retained something of the Mitteleuropa of its beginnings, with its royal palace, buildings from the 1900s and its numerous parks, in the middle of which are monuments from its varied past—medieval churches, Turkish mosques and buildings from the Communist era.

The vast **St Alexander Nevsky Square**, with its cathedral towering above it in the centre, is where Sofia was reborn at the end of the 19th century. All the great national buildings rise up around it: the National Assembly, Academy of Sciences, National Library and the University. The **Cathedral** was consecrated in 1912 in memory of the Bulgarian, Russian, Finnish and Romanian soldiers who died in the war of liberation against the Ottoman Empire from 1877 to 1878. Its name honours the patron saint of Russia's Tsar Alexander II. The monumental sanctuary, crowned with gilded cupolas and comprising a nave and four aisles, is reminiscent of the grandiose and massive style prevalent at the time in St Petersburg. Some 200 icons are displayed in the crypt.

The eternal flame of the monument to the Unknown Soldier faces the Cathedral and points the way to the **St Sophia Basilica**. Restored in 1998, this austere brick edifice is one of the oldest in Sofia.

Tsar Osvoboditel Boulevard, main thoroughfare of the town's historic centre, runs straight east-west between the University and the TZUM Central Department Store. The capital's major centres of interest surround this area.

A vast esplanade with shady gardens, **Kniaz Alexander Battenberg Square** is the true heart of

the city. Ivan Bazov National
Theatre, built by Austrian
architects in 1907, dominates the
square with its neoclassical
pediment and two neo-baroque
tower decorated with statues of
the goddess Athena Nike.

The fine creamy yellow façade
of the neo-baroque Royal Palace
opens out onto the esplanade. It
was built in 1889 as a home for
Prince Alexander Battenberg
after his election. Today, it
houses the **National Art Gallery**,
exhibiting collections of
Bulgarian art from the Middle
Ages to the present day, and the
National Ethnographic Museum,
displaying jewellery, craftwork,
costumes, embroidery, carpets
and furniture.

The **Archaeological Museum**,
just west of the square, is
housed in the Great Mosque
(Büyük camii) built by the Turks
in the late 15th century. Its
collections trace the history of
the country from its origins to the
Middle Ages. The finest pieces
are on the ground floor, devoted
to classical antiquity and the
Early Christian era. The most
renowned exhibit is the Thracian
treasure of Valchitran,
comprising 13 pieces in 12.5 kg
of pure gold.

Facing the museum, the
presidential offices are guarded
by two soldiers in ceremonial

hemis.fr/Guy

Alexander Nevsky Cathedral.

white uniform with scarlet collar
and an ostrich-feathered *kalpak*
fur hat. The grand changing of
the guard takes place at 10 a.m.
with simpler versions performed
every hour. Beyond the main
entrance you can see in the
middle of the great courtyard
Sofia's most ancient edifice, the
St George Rotunda, a round red-
brick church original built at the
end of the Roman Empire, probably in the 4th century.

Vitocha Boulevard, a bustling
shopping street, is lined with
several fashionable boutiques
and extends towards the
monumental Communist-era
Palace of Culture.

stone into bizarre gigantic pillars. To control the Balkan passage, the Romans built a guard-post in the 1st century as an eyrie up in a striking ensemble of towering rocks, a wildly romantic fort which Turks and Bulgars subsequently took over.

Lom

Lom (km 743) is Bulgaria's second-largest Danube port, after Ruse. It was built on the site of a Roman fortification, Almus. Finds from Roman times can be seen in the town's museum.

On the Romanian side, the river flows past a long stretch of lakes, teeming with fish.

Kozloduj

The next Bulgarian town of importance is Kozloduj (km 700), with its nuclear power station.

The town was the site of a dramatic incident in 1876. The 28-year-old Bulgarian poet and freedom fighter Christo Botev forced the captain of the Danube steamer *Radetzky* to moor here, so that he and his 200 followers could take up the fight against the Turks. Shortly afterwards he and his comrades-in-arms lost their lives, but to this day their act of bravery is commemorated by flowers laid on the river bank, spelling out Botev's initials in Cyrillic script.

Orjahovo

High up in a picturesque landscape of cornfields and vineyards, the town of Orjahovo (km 678) is an agricultural centre.

Gigen

Near to the small port of Bajkal at the mouth of the Iskar (km 636),

important finds from Roman times were unearthed at Gigen. The foundations of a large temple, precious mosaics, paved streets, water mains and sewers indicate that this was the site of the Roman town of **Ulpia Escus**.

On the Romanian bank, you pass by **Corabia** (km 630), a centre for sugar refinery. Mineral oil is trans-shipped in the Bulgarian town of **Somovit** (km 608).

Nikopol

Nikopol (km 597) also looks back to a Roman past. Trajan achieved a major victory over the Dacians here and named the fort "Town of the Victory on the Lower Danube" (Nicopolis ad Istrum). In 629 the Byzantine Emperor Heraclius had the fortress extended. The Turks strengthened it further, but in 1810 the Russians pulled down the massive fortifications. The ruins are still worth a visit, and you might also like to peep into the small 13th-century church nearby.

Pleven

From here you can take an overland trip to Pleven, the biggest and most important town on the Danube plain—and one of the most ancient. It was settled in prehistoric times (4th to 3rd millennium BC), and then variously held, much later, by the Thracians, Romans, Slavs and Turks. Several churches are worth a visit, as are the History Museum and Skobelev Park, where the historic battle for Pleven (1877), which played a central role in Bulgaria's fight for independence against the Turks, is depicted

realistically in a circular panorama. The mausoleum in the city centre commemorates the Russian and Romanian troops who fell in 1877.

Pleven's centre may surprise you with its well-kept bourgeois buildings in the pedestrian zone, as well as its large park full of fountains and artificial waterfalls.

Turnu Măgurele

Opposite Nikopol and linked by ferry is the port and fertilizer factory of Turnu Măgurele, with its population of about 30,000.

Belene Island

Between km 577 and km 560, you pass by the Bulgarian island of Belene, whose once infamous concentration camp for political prisoners is not visible from the river. Work on a nuclear power plant has been frozen. The island is part of Persina Natural Park.

Svištov

At Svištov (km 554), the Danube approaches its southernmost point. The terraced layout of the town on the hilly banks above the river gives it a particular charm. Among the sights in this major port are two unusual 17th-century underground churches, as well as the Holy Trinity Church and a museum dedicated to the Bulgarian writer Alek Konstantinov, shot dead in 1897, aged 34.

Veliko Tarnovo

Excursions also go to picturesque Veliko Tarnovo, medieval capital of Bulgaria (1187–1396), also known as the City of the Tsars. It is almost encircled by the Yantra river, the houses clinging to the steep sides of the gorge. Watching over it all, the Zarevez fortress stands on a spectacular peninsula enclosed by a meander of the river. Easy to defend, the site was occupied by the Thracians, then by all the other tribes that ruled Bulgaria. In the 12th century, two boyar brothers, Asen and Peter, declared the end of Byzantine rule in Bulgaria and proclaimed the city a capital. The tsar and the patriarchs settled in the fortress, the nobles on the hill facing it, while the merchants and craftsmen resided in the lower town. Tarnovo soon became one of the main political and cultural centres of eastern Europe, renowned for its art school. The Turks took the city in 1393, putting an end to its golden age. But its medieval atmosphere remains. The shops along the cobbled streets around Samovodska Charshiya are a delight. Apart from the lovely old houses, there are several museums and churches to be seen.

Arbanassi

The ruins of the stronghold on Zarevez hill are best observed from the nearby village of Arbanassi, less than 10 minutes' drive away. It has been listed by UNESCO as a World Heritage site for the originality of its fortified houses and the beauty of the frescoes in the Nativity church, the best-known of the five churches built in the 16th and 17th centuries. Arbanassi Palace, now a 5-star boutique hotel, was the residence of the last communist dictator Todor Jivkov.

Ruse

Ruse (km 495), with 157,000 inhabitants, is Bulgaria's biggest Danube port. Back when the Roman fleet was stationed here, the place was called Sextanta Prista ("Sixty Ships"). A new settlement under the name of Ruse (or Rousse) is first mentioned at the beginning of the 16th century; the Turks later named it Ruschuk. In the 19th century the city experienced an upturn in its fortunes: the first railway in the Ottoman Empire (from Ruschuk to Varna on the Black Sea) was opened here.

Little of historical interest has survived, although the neobaroque buildings in the city centre give Ruse the appearance of

www.velikoturnovo.info

Claude Hervé-Bazir

Serbian National Tourist Board

Picturesque Veliko Tarnovo. | Roses are one of Bulgaria's main exports. | The extraordinary sandstone pillars of Belogradchik.

an old Austrian provincial town. Sights include the Holy Trinity Church (*Sveta Troiza*) of 1764 with its beautiful icons and frescoes, and the National Theatre (1891). The railway station is the largest and considered the finest in the country. Opposite the Hotel Riga, the Urban Lifestyle of Ruse Museum occupies the handsome wooden Kaliopa House.

For rest and recreation, the inhabitants of this industrial town have many parks to choose from, as well as the **Lipnik Nature Reserve** 12 km (7.5 miles) away. Another worthwhile excursion is to the cliff monasteries of Ivanovo (12th–15th centuries) with their unique murals, listed by UNESCO.

Giurgiu

The only Danube bridge between Romania and Bulgaria is the 2224-m **Friendship Bridge** (km 489) built in 1954. Trains travel over the steel structure into the Romanian town of Giurgiu (km 493) on the lower level and cars on the upper level. The name originates from Genoese sailors who built a trading station and a castle, San Giorgio, here in the 14th century. Of the great Turkish fortress only a lopsided watchtower in the town centre remains.

Many of the 70,000 residents of this industrial town and centre for the surrounding agricultural area commute to the Romanian capital.

Bucharest

Most people landing in Giurgiu do not stay in town but head for Bucharest, 64 km away. Bucharest is the political, economical and cultural centre of the country,

in the heart of Walachia. The city spreads along the banks of the Dâmboviţa, a tributary of the Danube, and the first written documents mentioning the city were signed by Prince Vlad Ţepeş, "the Impaler", ruler of Walachia and model for Dracula, on September 20, 1459.

Over the centuries the city endured several dark periods and catastrophic events, notably its destruction by the Turks in 1595. In 1659, it became capital of Walachia and then, two centuries later (1862), of the principality formed by the reunion of Walachia and Moldavia. It was designated capital of the Kingdom of Romania in 1881.

During its golden age, between the two world wars, the city was redesigned by French and Romanian architects trained in Paris.

The streets were transformed into tree-lined boulevards, a triumphal arch was erected, earning Bucharest the title of "Little Paris of the East".

Of Romania's 21 million inhabitants, 1.9 million live in Bucharest, most of them in the wide belt of faceless apartment buildings encircling the city centre. The vast majority (87 per cent) are Orthodox, devoutly so.

After the revolution that brought Romania to the international headlines in December 1989, the people are still trying to find their feet. They survived the hardships imposed by Nicolae Ceauşescu's personality cult, thanks to their self-deprecating sense of humour and an ability to always manage, somehow. You'll find them cheerful and friendly, and eager to talk to strangers.

Claude Hervé-Bazin

Since Romania joined the EU in 2007, life has changed considerably, though incomes remain low compared with other EU countries.

Around Bulevardul Unirii

Start your sightseeing in Old Bucharest at Piaţa Unirii. The square is about two-thirds of the way along Bulevardul Unirii, the senselessly long fountain-studded avenue culminating in Ceauşescu's huge palace. Look along the esplanade covering the river, lined with boutiques and shopping centres. This was the former Avenue of the Victory of Socialism, 100 m wide, which the citizens referred to as Kitsch Boulevard during Ceauşescu's rule. At the far western end of the avenue is the enormous **Parliament Palace** *(Palatul Parlamentului)*, the house that Ceauşescu built. Perched on top of an artificial hill riddled with secret passages and anti-atomic shelters, it is something of a national embarrassment. A fantasy of marble and gilt, it has 1100 rooms (second in size only to the Pentagon), secret passageways and nuclear shel-

Claude Hervé-Bazin

The Dâmboviţa is a canalized tributary of the Danube. | In the Lipscani Quarter, Zlătari Church, built in 1837, is reflected in the glass façade of a modern bank.

ters. To clear away the area for its construction, 40,000 inhabitants were displaced and a fifth of the old town was destroyed, including 19 churches, 9 of which were listed historic monuments. Inside, the floors are marble, the walls lined with walnut and cherry panelling, the ceilings six storeys high. The infamous Ceauşescu couple never had time to enjoy their palace; it was still unfinished when they were executed in 1989. At present it is the seat of parliament and congress centre.

The Old Trading District
The most important sights of Bucharest are north of the Dâm bovița, particularly in the area bounded by Calea Victoriei and the parallel Bulevardul Magheru.

In the 16th and 17th centuries the **Lipscani Quarter** was the city centre; the name came from the city of Leipzig, as many goods were imported from there. Its southern boundary is the Dâmbovița, in the west Calea Victoriei and in the north boulevards Regina Elisabeta and Carol I, while in the east it stops at Bulevardul Bratianu. Many small shops have appeared among the old baroque buildings.

Curtea Veche
Near Piața Unirii stand the remains of Curtea Veche (Old Courtyard), the palace of Vlad Țepeș, residence of the princes of Walachia and the only vestige of the medieval city. It was built in the 15th century and expanded by Constantin Brancovan (1688–1714). Destroyed by fire and earthquake, it was abandoned in the 18th century. Little remains of the grand vaulted halls and the luxuriant gardens.

The **church of Curtea Veche** *(Biserica Curtea Veche),* on Iuliu Manui street, was founded in the middle of the 16th century during the reign of Prince Mircea Ciobanu. The Walachian princes were sworn in here. Opposite, Hanul lui Manuc is an inn built round a central courtyard by an Armenian merchant in 1808.

Around Stavropoleos Church
Bucharest is graced by numerous churches; perhaps the most attractive is located just north of Piața Unirii. On the corner of the same name, Stavropoleos Church *(Biserica Stavropoleos)* was built in 1724 when Bucharest was governed by a Phanariot from Constantinople. Oriental influence is evident in the arabesques and arcades; the frescoes, portraits of saints, are painted in the icon style, with gold leaf. Generally the churches are only open during services (which are frequent). Try the door, you might be in luck. In the same street, opposite the church, stands the old brasserie

Carul cu Bere (literally, Beer Wagon), worth visiting just for its exuberant décor of painted woodwork, arched vaulting, frescoes and stained-glass windows.

A short walk away, at the crossroads with Calea Victoriei, stands a pompous building that houses the **National History Museum** *(Muzeul Naţional de Istorie a României)*. It was originally the post office, built in neoclassical style in 1900. Among the many thousands of exhibits, the most interesting are the Daco-Roman collections, and the Treasury, presenting gold pieces from simple neolithic pieces to intricate Transylvanian jewellery of the 16th and 17th centuries.

Close by, **Pasajul Villacros**, a glass-roofed shopping arcade, stretches between Victoriei and Carada streets. It opens onto the National Bank, a fine neoclassical colonnaded affair taking up a whole block. Further north is the baroque **National Library** *(Biblioteca Naţională)* and in Strada Ion Ghica, the Russian-Orthodox **church of St Nicholas** *(Biserica Rusă)* with its onion domes (1905–09). On Bratianu Avenue, the little Şuţu Palace, a handsome neo-Gothic building enhanced by a wrought-iron and glass porch, was built from 1833 to 1835 for a Marshal of the court. It now houses the **Municipal Museum of Art and History** *(Muzeul municipiului)*, tracing the development of the capital in photographs and other displays.

From Piaţa Universitatii to the North

Piaţa Universitatii is one of the busiest squares of the city, dominated by the tower of the Inter-Continental Hotel and the modern **National Theatre** *(Teatrul Naţional)*. West of the square is the Second-Empire style university building and, in Enei Street, the neo-Byzantine façade of the Ion Mincu Institute of Architecture. Many hotels, theatres and public buildings populate the district to the north in the streets around Calea Victoriei.

Walking up Calea Victoriei you will see, on the left, the red-brick Creţulescu Church, topped by two domes. Immediately behind it, on Revolution Square, is the imposing neoclassical building of the **National Museum of Art of Romania** *(Muzeul Naţional de Artă al României)* on the corner of Strada Ştirbei Vodă. The building is the former Palace of the Republic, much damaged during the December Revolution, when the collections were severely depleted. Paintings by Romanian and European artists are displayed, in addition to works from the Far East.

Opposite stands the Central University Library with its neoclassical columns. On the same side of the street, the imposing **Ateneul Român**, beneath a great dome, was built between 1886 and 1888 by a French architect.

At the northern end of Calea Victoriei is the eclectic Cantacuzino Palace (1898) housing the **George Enescu Museum** (*Muzeul Naţional George Enescu*).

To Herăstrău Park

The majestic Şoseaua Kiseleff Boulevard, shaded by tall trees, leads north from Victoriei Square to the Triumphal Arch and Herăstrău Park. Along the way, don't miss the **Museum of the Romanian Peasant**, displaying traditional costumes, icons and cooking utensils from another era. The **Arcul de Triumf**, on the square of the same name, is similar to the one in Paris, but only half the size. It ws first built of wood in 1922, then in stone in 1935, to the memory of the soldiers of World War I.

Herăstrău Park, north of the Triumphal Arch, contains the fascinating **Muzeul Satului**, founded in 1936 by Dimitrie Gusti, a professor of sociology. Called the Village and Folk Art Museum, it

Romanian woodcarving: an old window preserved in the Village and Folk Art Museum; and a souvenir for tourists, the inevitable Dracula.

Frédérique Fasser

Claude Hervé-Bazin

Danube Writers. Panait Istrati (1884–1935) was the son of a Greek smuggler in Brăila. He led an adventurous life and celebrated the magic of the Baragan steppes and the banks of the Danube writing mostly in French, a language which he had taught himself. Elias Canetti (1905–94) describes his birthplace, Ruse, which at that time still went by its Turkish name, in his autobiography: "Ruschuk [...] was a marvellous town [...], inhabited by people of the most varied origins; on any one day you could hear seven or eight languages spoken." In his childhood, the main languages were Spanish, his mother tongue, and Bulgarian; he used German to write his books, for which he was awarded the Nobel Prize in 1981.

assembles 300 wooden buildings brought here from the four corners of Romania—farms, barns, thatched cottages, chalets, shepherd's huts, chapels, wells and windmills, all with their furnishings, bed linen, tablecloths, icons, down to the pots of basil on the windowsill.

Cotroceni Palace

On Bulevardul Geniului in the west part of the city, in a magnificent setting of wooded gardens, the Cotroceni Palace was built in 1893 by a French architect for Princess Marie, granddaughter of Queen Victoria and wife of King Ferdinand of Romania. It is partly open to the public, used for concerts and houses a museum displaying interesting medieval collections, as well as the residence of the President of the Republic.

Behind the palace, the **Botanical Garden** (Gradina Botanică) was created in 1884–85 and covers 17 ha planted with species from the world over.

Oltenița

The industrial and warehouse town of Oltenița (km 430) serves as a residence for commuters to the capital, just as ship passengers use it as a starting point or destination for Bucharest excursions.

Tutrakan

Opposite, the Bulgarian town of Tutrakan, is an important fisheries centre and was already a stronghold back in Roman times.

Srebarna Biosphere Reserve

Bird spotters take up positions on the heights of the Danube island of Vetren (km 358) to look out for rare species heading for the 9-sq-km reserve. Among the breeders are the curly-feathered Dalmatian pelicans, six varieties of heron, including the purple and squacco herons. Various kites and falcons can be seen circling overhead and numerous species of duck nest or spend the winter in the nature reserve protected around Lake Srebarna since 1942.

Silistra

Silistra (km 376), close to the Bulgarian-Romanian border, was founded by Trajan in the 2nd century. In 1942 a Roman tomb was discovered here with very beautiful, well-preserved mural paintings from the 4th century, depicting scenes of family life, hunting, plants and birds. The old Turkish fortress of Silistra has also resisted the ravages of time.

Negotiating the narrow waterways of the
Danube Delta.

To the Delta

From km 374 the Danube flows entirely through Romanian territory for the next 240 km.

Dobrogea and Baragan

On the right bank begins the Dobrogea plateau, stretching all the way to the Black Sea; the Baragan plain on the left bank is reminiscent of the Hungarian puszta. The bygone romanticism of this steppe landscape has been captured in the books of the Romanian writer Panait Istrati (see p. 96).

Braţul Borcea

At km 371, the Danube divides into two arms, the Braţul Borcea (Borcea arm) and the main river, coming together again at km 248 to embrace the Balta Ialomiţei island area. The 100-km Braţul Borcea is deeper and 23 km shorter than the main river, with both routes serving ship traffic. From Călăraşi (km 97 of the Braţul Borcea) a ferry sails to the Bulgarian town of Silistra and a Romanian ferry serves Ostrov (km 367).

Adamclisi

From Ostrov, the road snakes through a beautiful area to Adamclisi, where a Roman memorial, the Tropaeum Trajani, commemorates Trajan's decisive victory over the Dacians. It is a large, circular building with a frieze of rectangular panels, each depicting figures of Romans or their enemies, carved by legionary troops.

To Constanţa

The road continues through the vineyards of Murfatlar, which produce a sweet white dessert wine of the same name, to reach Constanţa, Romania's biggest port on the Black Sea. This is also the terminus of the 64-km (40-mile) Danube Canal, completed in 1983, which starts in Cernavodă.

Cernavodă

Back to the river. In Cernavodă (km 300), which means "Black Water", the Danube is at its closest to the Black Sea. Another great feat of engineering is the railway bridge built in 1895, which over a distance of 15 km crosses the Danube, Ialomiţa Island and the Braţul Borcea as far as Feteşti (km 36 of the Braţul Borcea). It was a significant aid in the economic development of the Danubian region. Today, the two towns are also linked by motorway.

Ghindăreşti

After Cernavodă the river turns northwards. On the right bank, Ghindăreşti (km 260) comes into view, a small, old Russian fishing

village in a very picturesque location. The domes of the Orthodox church have a silvery gleam.

Hârşova

Like most places on the lower Danube, Hârşova (km 253) was a Roman camp and later a Turkish fortress. The fine Russian Orthodox church was founded by the Lipovan sect, which is now mainly to be found in the delta.

After the River Ialomiţa flows into the Braţul Borcea, the latter joins up again with the main river. The Danube Valley narrows for a few kilometres.

Today, a road bridge heading for Giurgeni on the left bank crosses the river at km 238; in earlier times, shepherds from Transylvania used to cross here to graze their flocks on the fertile Dobrogea plain.

Brăila

After the narrows, the river divides up again and forms a 60-km-long landscape of islands and beds of reeds, the Balta Brăila, reuniting with the Danube at Brăila itself (km 170). This port, which was first mentioned in 1368, was fought over fiercely in the Middle Ages. For almost 300 years it was defended by a Turkish fortress, finally pulled down in 1829. Today Brăila is home to various industries; the reeds from the Danube delta are processed here. Brăila is the birthplace of the Romanian writer Panait Istrati, son of a laundress and a Greek smuggler. He published in French; his best-known work is *The Confession of a Loser* (see p. 96).

Galaţi

At Galaţi (km 150), between the mouths of the two large tributaries Siretul and Prut, the Danube makes its last decisive turn to the east. The town was founded 500 years ago but it doesn't look its age, for heavy damage in World War II left nothing of the old centre. As in Brăila, all life centres round the harbour, which has a large shipyard.

Along the lower reaches of the Prut runs the border between Romania and Moldova, formed as an independent republic in 1991. From its mouth at km 134 for about half a kilometre, the two countries share a common Danube border. So at km 133, the left bank is already part of Ukraine, and for the next 53 km, the Danube forms the Ukrainian-Romanian border.

Reni

The next sizeable town, Reni (km 128), is an important Ukrainian commercial port. On the right bank you will pass by the former Turkish fortress of **Isaccea** (km 103). Its name derives from the

istockphoto.com/F. Kienas

Romanian Tourist Office

Romanian Tourist Office

Turkish Isak-Kioi ("Isaac's Village"). Honey is harvested from bees that feed in the extensive linden woodlands of the region; tobacco cultivation, wine-making and fishing are other important sources of income.

The Delta

The Danube delta is a world apart. To this day, barely a road crosses this watery kingdom, and the only way to explore the streams, the waterlily-carpeted lakes and the lonely fishing villages is by boat.

In the delta the Danube splits into three main branches or arms *(braţul)*: to the north the Chilia, which for almost its entire length forms the border between Ukraine and Romania, in the middle the canalized Sulina branch, the main thoroughfare for shipping traffic, and in the south the Sfântu Gheorghe branch, the oldest and most unspoilt.

The vast delta is shared between Romania, which owns four-fifths of the area, and Ukraine. With the immense lagoons of Razim and Sinoie, it covers more than 5000 sq km

This part of the world has hardly changed in 100 years. | Two members of the delta bird-world: a family of pelicans and a grey heron. Don't forget your binoculars.

Animal Kingdom. Tulcea and Vilkovo are the usual starting points for excursions into the delta to see its flora and fauna, unique in Europe.

In the marshes, there are eight different members of the heron family alone, including grey, purple and great white herons, little egrets and bitterns, as well as Dalmatian and white pelicans, storks, ibises, spoonbills and white-tailed eagles. Cormorants perch on the bank, drying their wings.

The land-based fauna include wildcats, wolves, wild boar, foxes and otters. The waters teem with fish, which form the staple diet of the human and animal inhabitants: pike, carp, pike-perch, catfish, tench, perch and bream, and sturgeon regularly swim up from the Black Sea. But freshwater herring are the fisherman's most important catch.

Romanian Tourist Office

(over 1900 sq miles), of which half are protected as a Biosphere Reserve.

The silt carried by the current has created a labyrinth of channels, nearly 400 lakes, spongy islands *(plauri)*, meadows and dunes linked by a vast network of canals. In some places you'll see elevated grinds, plateaux formed by deposits where trees have taken root. Reeds are everywhere and serve a useful purpose: they filter the polluted waters coming from upstream. A transition between the earth, the river and the sea, the immense delta, at the confluence of five migratory routes, is also the refuge of some 300 species of birds.

Here and there, you will see tiny villages of reed-thatched houses, blending in perfectly with their surroundings and accessible only by boat. For several days each spring, the river floods, the water seeping through the doorways and carrying away stabilized lands.

The 15,000 inhabitants of the delta live mostly from collecting reeds, fish farming and traditional fishing. In majority they are Lipovans, followers of the old Orthodox rites who fled here from Russia in the 17th century in the face of persecution by the Orthodox Church. They are generally known as Old Believers. Their churches often hold precious icons of limewood (*lipa* in Russian), and their traditional costumes and customs give the visitor a vivid impression of life in old Russia. They number more than 35,000 in Romania; they cross themselves with two fingers instead of three, and the men wear long beards.

Tulcea

The largest town of the delta, with a population of 91,000, lies just before the last fork in the Danube at km 71, on the site of the ancient Roman settlement of Aegissus, built in turn on a Dacian city founded in the 7th century BC. It is a significant port and industrial centre, with no particular charm, but the harbour bustles with luxury boats taking visitors on trips into the delta.

In town, you can get a good overview of the many varieties of local flora and fauna in the Danube Delta Museum, along with displays illlustrating the traditional life of delta fishermen. There are also museums of history and archaeology, folk art and ethnography, as well as an art gallery.

Bratul Sulina

Downstream from Tulcea, passenger boats ply back and forth incessantly between fishing craft and rusting cargoes along the Sulina branch. The channel was deepened back in the 19th century to permit the passage of bigger ships, and the winding 92-km stretch of river was turned into a 64-km canal with a navigable channel 150 m wide and at least 7.50 m deep. Merchandise and passengers are unloaded at regular intervals outside the little villages scattered along the banks.

Via **Crişan**, one of the largest fishing villages in the delta, you reach the port of **Sulina**, where the Danube flows into the Black Sea. You can see the 0-km marker near the old lighthouse. Already a settlement in Byzantine times, Sulina was later a mooring point for Genoese ships. Since the 19th-century, this former fishing village has developed shipyards and a fish-processing industry. Here, the work of the river is highlighted: by depositing 80 million tons of silt and gaining 40 m from the sea each year, it has moved the lighthouse from the shore to the middle of the marketplace! From here the Black Sea seems just a stone's throw away, even if ships still have to journey another 12 km through a canal bordered by quays in order to reach the open sea.

Bratul Sfântu Gheorghe

At the mouth of the southernmost of the three arms, Sfântu Gheorghe is the headquarters of the

sturgeon fishermen. Bratul Sfântu Gheorghe traces great loops until it reaches the Black Sea.

Braţul Chilia

The northernmost branch, Chilia, is in places over 1000 m wide. Alone it carries two-thirds of the river waters to the delta. It is longer (120 km) and more tortuous than the others, and dotted with islands, and was long ignored because it marked the boundary with the Soviet Union. At its mouth, it breaks up into myriad mini-deltas.

At km 90 lies **Izmaïl**. The earliest settlers here were probably Scythians, followed by Greeks, Romans and Slavs. From the 15th century onwards, the fortress was the focus of bitter fighting between the Russians and Turks. In 1790 the Russian generals Suvorov and Kutuzov succeeded in capturing the town. Suvorov is commemorated by an equestrian statue and a museum. Afterwards the town was passed back and forth between Romania, Russia and Moldova, to finally become part of independent Ukraine in 1991.

Vilkovo (Vylkove in Ukrainian), the main Lipovan town (km 14), was founded in the 18th century by Cossacks. The inhabitants live from fishing and winemaking.

Cocos Monastery, 30 km west of Tulcea. | **Ukraine: a kobza-player.**

CONSTANŢA (CONSTANZA)

The Romanian Black Sea coast stretches over 240 km between the Danube delta in the north and the Bulgarian frontier in the south. The hinterland, bounded to the west by the river, forms the Dobrogea plain, with an almost Mediterranean climate.

Constanţa is one of the country's principal cities and its biggest commercial sea port. When it was founded, under the name Tomis, Greek traders came to exchange their wines for Dacian grain. But the city reached its height under the Romans, when it became the main port of the Black Sea. During the reign of Augustus, the poet Ovid spent his last years here, in exile. After the fall of the Roman empire, and numerous barbarian invasions, the city sank into oblivion. Much later, around 1300, the Genoese built a harbour, and a new era of prosperity began. During the four centuries of Ottoman rule the city foundered once again, until 1878 when Dobrogea was united with Romania.

On Piaţa Ovidiu (Ovid Square), site of the agora of ancient Tomis, stands a statue of the author of the *Metamorphoses*. The **Archaeological Museum**, in the old town hall, displays a collection of Greco-Roman objects: gold jewellery, coins, bas-reliefs, fine glassware, pottery and marbles, including a strange depiction of the Glycon, a snake-god with a half-human, half-equine head associated with the cult of Asclepius. Behind the museum, a glass building protects one of the biggest mosaics of Europe (4th century), 40 m long, with floral and geometrical patterns.

A few streets to the northwest, the **Archaeological Park** is strewn with vestiges of ancient buildings.

Down from Ovid Square you can see the slender minaret of the **Great Mosque**, built in 1910 on the ruins of the 1822 Mahmudia Mosque. If the door is open, you can climb up to get a fantastic view over the town and port. The interior is finely decorated in blue and ochre, and richly carpeted.

To the south is the Orthodox **cathedral** (19th-century). On the sea front, opposite the little aquarium, stands a big white Art Nouveau **Casino** (1907–10). Further north is the start of **Plaja Moderna**, one of the best beaches of the Romanian coast.

Spicy Serbian fish soup cooked on an open fire, and eaten outdoors—what could be better?

DINING OUT

Your Danube cruise will take you on a culinary voyage of discovery. After the hearty dishes of Germany you enter the realm of Austrian cutlets and dumplings, cream-drenched cakes and pastries. Things spice up in Slovakia and Hungary with their homely stews, while Bulgarians sing the praises of their yoghurt, and Serbia and Romania have many tasty surprises in store.

Austria

The emperors and archdukes have gone; not so the Bohemian dumplings, Hungarian goulash, Polish stuffed cabbage and Serbian *shashlik*. But there are Austrian specialities too: *Wienerschnitzel*, a thinly sliced cutlet of veal sauteed in a coating of egg and breadcrumbs; *Backhendl*, boned deep-fried chicken prepared like *Wienerschnitzel*; *Tafelspitz*, boiled beef, a Viennese favourite; or *Knödel*, dumplings served with soups and with the meat dish, studded with pieces of liver or bacon. Other main courses you'll find include roast meats (*Rostbraten*) with garlic, and in rural areas *Bauernschmaus*, literally "farmer's feast". With the Danube on the doorstep, fish turns up on many menus: trout, zander (pikeperch), pike and carp are prepared in various tasty ways.

Dumplings are also served as a dessert with hot apricot inside (*Marillenknödel*) or with cream cheese (*Topfenknödel*). As for

Yoghurt. The Bulgarians will not have it any other way: they insist that they invented yoghurt! According to legend, a shepherd of Stara Planina ran out of buckets to collect the milk of his ewes, and poured it into a new goatskin bag. The next morning, he discovered the milk transformed into yoghurt, thanks to a local bacteria, *Lactobacillus bulgaricus*. Some claim that yoghurt was already known to the nomadic Hunno-Bulgars who began migrating into Europe in the 2nd century. Others say that it has its origins in Central Asia, though don't try telling that to the Bulgarians, who believe it helps them live longer.

pastries, the variations of cherries, strawberries, hazelnuts, walnuts, apple and chocolate in tarts, pies, cakes and strudels are endless, and they are all even better topped with whipped cream (*mit Schlag*). And you can join in the never-ending controversy over the famous chocolate cake, the Sachertorte—whether it should be split and sandwiched together with apricot jam, or just left plain.

The local wines are mostly white, and people are happy to drink white wine with either meat or fish. The best known, Gumpoldskirchner, has the full body and bouquet of its southern vineyards, but Grinzinger, Sieveringer and Neustifter are equally popular. From the Danube valley, with an extra natural sparkle, come the Kremser, Dürnsteiner and Langenloiser. One way to enjoy them is to visit a *Heuriger*, where you drink young white wine and help yourself to a buffet of hot and cold snacks, usually including cheese, cold meats and salads.

Bulgaria

Centuries of Turkish domination have left their mark on Bulgarian cuisine, in such dishes as *kyopolou*, a dip made from roasted and pureed aubergine (eggplant), pepper stuffed with minced meat, and kebabs (here spelt *kebap*) of beef or pork. *Banitza* is a baked cheese pastry, and *moussaka* is much like that made by Greek and Turkish neighbours. The spinach and zucchini soups are delicious, and Bulgaria claims to be the home of the world's best, most authentic and health-giving yoghurts.

The best Bulgarian wines, especially the rich reds, have made themselves an international reputation. Some of the best are made in Bordeaux style, from cabernet sauvignon and merlot grapes, but look also for the full-bodied local varietals *mavrud* and *melnik*, and the lighter *gamza*.

Croatia

The dishes you will be offered in Croatia vary greatly with the region. Along the Danube they reflect past periods of Turkish, Hungarian and Austrian influence, as in neighbouring Serbia. The cured, dried or smoked hams and salami-like sausage are excellent. You might be offered *burek*, a meat pie made from beef and onions, stews of sausage and beans, and for dessert, *Bregovska pita*, a delicious version of Viennese apple strudel.

Very drinkable red and white wines come from the Croatia's Dalmatian coast and offshore islands, and the locals regard no occasion as complete without a shot or two of *šljivovica*, plum brandy.

Germany

Traditional German food relies heavily on soups, stews, roasts and many varieties of sausage. The Danube flows through Bavaria, known for its beer and for its *Weisswürste*, white veal sausages flavoured with pepper and onions and served with sweet mustard. The locals like to eat them as a midday snack before starting on a proper lunch. Try also *Blaue Zipfel*, finger-sized sausages poached with onions in vinegar, and grilled *Bratwürste*. A favourite soup is *Leberknödelsuppe*, liver dumplings in beef bouillon. Main dishes include *Kalbsvögerl*, veal roll stuffed with onion, morel mushrooms, garlic and sour cream, and *Schweinebraten*, roast pork with herbs.

Succumb to desserts such as *Schmarren*, baked pancakes with apples and raisins, and *Zwetschgendatschi*, pastry with plums, cinnamon and sugar.

Germany's wines, predominantly white, are many and varied and to foreigners may seem confusingly named. But among them there is something to suit most tastes, whether as an apéritif or to go with dinner. Franconia, the

A varied menu: Hungarian goulasch; Viennese schnitzel; excellent wines from Serbia; jam-filled, trellised Linzertorte.

istockphoto.com//zso

Österreich Werbung

Serbian National Tourist Board

Touristinenformation Linz

region around Würzburg and Bamberg, produces fresh white wines to put in its famous bockbeutel, round-bellied bottles.

Hungary

A popular appetizer is *libamáj-pástétom*, flaky pastry filled with goose-liver pâté. *Hortobágyi húsos palacsinta* are pancakes filled with minced meat and sour cream; *gombafejek rántva*, breadcrumb-coated fried mushrooms. Now for the goulash, which is not at all a spicy stew, but a thinnish soup. Called *gulyásleves*, it combines bits of beef, vegetables, caraway seeds and paprika for colour and zing. *Szegedi halászlé* is a freshwater fish soup.

For the fish course, try *paprikás ponty*, carp with paprika sauce; *rácponty*, carp stew with sour cream; or *pisztráng tejszín mártásbán*, baked trout with cream.

Hungarians are extremely fond of large helpings of meat. *Pörkölt* or *bográcsgulyás* is the spicy stew that non-Hungarians call goulash. On menus you'll see *paprikás csirke*, chicken with sour cream and paprika. *Töltött paprika* are stuffed peppers; *bélszin Budapest módra* is a thick beef steak served with a sauce of peppers, mushrooms, peas and chopped chicken livers.

The Hungarians excel in the dessert department, so be sure to save room for a strudel *(rétes)* filled with *almás* (apple), *mákos* (poppy seeds), *meggyes* (sour cherries) or *túrós* (lemon, raisins and cottage cheese); or *Gundel palacsinta*, pancakes with a rich filling of chopped walnuts and raisins, covered in chocolate sauce and flambéed with brandy or rum.

Romania

Romanian cuisine can be fairly described as hearty. Staples are potatoes and a corn mash similar to Italian polenta *(mamaliga)*, while the star of the meat department is pork, usually in the form of chops or sausages. Food tends to be bland rather than spicy, and vegetarians will not have an easy time.

Lunch often consists of soup: *bortsch*, made from beetroot and giblets; sour-tasting *ciorba*, based on fermented bran, with various additions such as tripe, potatoes, marrow-bones or chicken; *colesa*, made from boletus mushrooms.

At dinner, a large dish of cold meats, liver pâté and salami is often served as hors-d'œuvre. The main course may be tasty *sarmalés*, cabbage leaves stuffed with minced beef and rice, braised until golden and served with *mamaliga*; then comes another hearty course of roast chicken *(pui)* with fried potatoes and a sauce of crushed garlic, vinegar and water, or grilled cutlets *(muschiu)* of pork *(porc)* or beef *(vaca)*, with tiny spicy pork sausages *(mititei)*.

Vegetables, served separately, are usually slices of aubergine or peppers braised in oil, or fat gherkins. Salads *(salata)* are rarely more varied than lettuce, tomato and cucumber.

Cheese is either yellow and compact *(cascaval)* or white and crumbly *(urda* or *brinza)*. Dessert may be fruit, ice cream, or, on special occasions, an elaborate gâteau with several layers of cream and frosted topping.

Meals might begin (and end) with a small glass of *tsuica*, a heady plum brandy to be downed in one gulp to the toast, *Noroc!* Red and white wines are produced in the country. The best reds come from Murfatlar near Constanza. The best whites are the dry traminer or riesling or the sweet *feteasca*, all from Cotnari. With their meals many Romanians tend to stick to the whites.

The beer *(bere)* is a light lager. Bottled mineral water, *apa minerale*, is slightly fizzy. Soft drinks are sold straight from the crate at street stalls.

Outside Budapest's most prestigious pastry shop, Café Gerbeaud. | A luscious display of vegetables in Vienna's Naschmarkt.

HUNGARIAN WINES

Hungary will keep the most demanding wine-lover in a state of bliss. It's a huge producer of quality wines, though few are household names abroad. The renowned Tokaji (or Tokay) as the jewel in its crown—the wine of kings and the king of wines. Made in the Tokaj region of the Northern Uplands, it uses native Furmint and Hárslevelü grapes and ranges from the pale, dry Tokaji Furmint to the rich amber Tokaji aszú dessert wine. The latter is one of the world's great sweet wines and has had its praises sung by Louis XIV, Beethoven, Schubert and Robert Browning. Its degree of sweetness is expressed in *puttonyos*, numbered from 3 to 6 (the sweetest) and indicating the quantity of baskets (*puttony*) of "noble" grapes added to each barrel of wine.

More popularly identified with Hungary is Bull's Blood from around Eger (Egri Bikavér), a red table wine whose name tells you all you need to know about its full-bodied character. It matches with Hungary's abundance of meaty dishes, as do the younger reds, Kékfrankos and Kékoportó, and the fine Villányi-Burgundi.

But most of the country's wines are white. To accompany Lake Balaton fish, you should try a Lake Balaton wine. From the vineyards around Badacsony, on the north shore, look for a range of white wines using well-known grape varieties, including Olaszrízling, a medium-bodied Riesling, Traminer and Pinot Blanc.

Huber/Pavan

Serbia

Serbian cuisine reflects the influence of many cultures: Turkish and Austro-Hungarian dishes feature on the menu alongside traditional local favourites.

Weather permitting, a leisurely meal on one of the many raft or river-boat restaurants at Zemun is a relaxing way to spend an evening. For music in an arty atmosphere, head for Skadarlija.

Pršut (cured ham) and *salama*, a kind of salami, make good starters, as does the winter *pasulj* (bean soup with smoked pork and peppers).

Main dishes are *ćevapčići* (grilled spicy fingers of minced meat), *pljeskavice* (meat patties), *ražnjići* (skewers of grilled meat, optionally served with sauerkraut), *sarma* (stuffed cabbage, vine leaves or peppers), *musaka* (oven-baked layers of minced meat and slices of potato, aubergine or courgettes), *gulaš*, a spicy stew with chunks of beef, onions and paprika, or *bečka šnicla* (Viennese breaded cutlet). A *šopska* or *srpska salata* (salad), sliced tomatoes and onion, sometimes cucumber and peppers, usually accompanies the main dish; out of season it may be pickles of various kinds. If you long for fresh perch from the Danube, then head for the Zemun quarter, known for its good fish restaurants.

If you have a sweet tooth, end your meal with a wedge of baklava, a flaky pastry filled with walnuts and oozing honey. *Palačinke* are pancakes with various fillings such as jam, chopped walnuts and chocolate sauce, or ice-cream. Poppy-seed strudel is another good dessert.

Sremski Karlovci, near Novi Sad, produces the country's best wines. To simplify communication with the waiter, learn the words *bjelo* for white, *crno* for red. The most famous spirits are *šljivovica* and *lozovača*, distilled from plums and grapes respectively.

Slovakia

In Bratislava's restaurants, you might try the local specialities: spicy beef goulash à la Bratislava or fiery shish kebabs with pork, beef and lamb (with ham, sausage, peppers and onions). With them come side dishes of vegetables and various potato concoctions including dumplings. *Loksa* are potato pancakes, often served with roast meats. Smoked cheese is another speciality, fried with ham and served with tartare sauce.

Local wines are mostly white, from the Veltliner, Sylvaner and Riesling grape varieties, and have sonorous names such as *Malokarpatské zlato* ("Gold from the Little Carpathians").

Bulgarian Damascus roses are distilled into essence and rosewater.

Corbis/Woolfitt

SHOPPING

There's no lack of opportunities for buying souvenirs of your trip, from Bulgarian rose water to Croatian designer fashions and Romanian lace. Fine crafts are available all along the Danube.

Austria

Not surprisingly, among the great attractions in Vienna—a city preoccupied by its history—are its antiques. Furniture and objets d'art from all over the old empire have somehow ended up here in the little shops in the Innere Stadt. Still in the realm of the past are the specialist coin-and stamp dealers (where else could you expect to find a wide selection of mint-condition pre-1914 Bosnia-Herzegovina and other imperial issues?).

The national Augarten porcelain workshops still turn out hand-decorated rococo chinaware. Exquisite petitpoint embroidery is available in the form of handbags, cushions and other items with flower, folk and opera motifs. You will find the more elegant shops on the Kärntnerstrasse, Graben and Kohlmarkt.

If your taste runs from the exquisite to kitsch, try your luck in the Saturday morning flea market on the Naschmarkt, with plenty of food stalls, too.

Craft products include pottery and jewellery. Small watercolours or copperplate engravings of the local landscape make a charming gift. Dolls in traditional costume are a popular buy, and a good bottle of local wine or apricot schnapps will go down well.

Bulgaria

Souvenirs and handicrafts in the markets, shops and roadside stalls include embroidered table cloths, costume jewellery, lace, dolls in regional folk costume, woven rugs, wooden toys, reproduction icons and paintings, as well as so-called antiques. There are also plenty of serious antique shops around which may hide a treasure or two, but check whether you require an export certificate before buying genuine antiques. You might also like to take home some Bulgarian wine, *rakia* (schnapps) sealed in ceramic urns, rose water, and some of the famous Troyan pottery, especially the casserole dishes which make excellent oven-to-table ware.

Österreich Werbung

Croatia

The range of crafts is more limited than in neighbouring countries, but you will find wooden toys, lace and embroidery and some attractive jewellery using silver and semi-precious stones. Croatia is clothes-conscious and a few of its designers have made a name for themselves internationally, so you may see something to suit you in the fashion boutiques. And did you know that the form of men's scarf called a cravat took its name from the Croats who wore it while serving as cavalrymen with various European armies over the centuries. Here you can buy the genuine article.

Germany

The shops are enticing, full of quality products beautifully displayed, whether it's food, clothing or the high-tech goods for which Germany is renowned. Toys are among the most attractive buys, from perfect replica trains and cars to charming dolls in regional folk costume. Fine porcelain is another speciality, both in reproductions of 18th-century pieces and in modern designs. Look in the museum shops for superb art books and lithographs.

Barbara Ender

Konstantin Kovačec

Sachertorte from Vienna. | **Romanian lace.** | **Petit-point tapestry.**

Hungary

Hungarian woodcarving is always popular—especially striking are Hussar chess sets painted in the bright colours of the famous brigade's uniforms. Falk Miksa utca is Budapest's main street for antique shops. Some other good buys include articles crafted from copper, brass or silver; leather goods; handmade carpets and rugs in traditional patterns; embroidered shirts, blouses and table linens. In food markets you will find sachets of ground paprika; spicy dried sausage; a garland of dried cherry peppers; packaged cake or strudel; a bottle of wine or fruit brandy. Music lovers will find a vast selection of CDs: Liszt, Kodály and Bartók, gypsy violins and folk music.

Romania

Traditional crafts have been maintained. Shops called Artizanat sell hand-embroidered table linen, but prices are high. The red woven scarves worn at Orthodox weddings make hard-wearing table runners or curtains. Other interesting buys are brightly painted woodcarvings, reproductions of icons and coloured ceramics.

Barbara Ender

istockphoto.com/G. Kenez

istockphoto.com/R. Razvan

Orthodox wedding scarf. | Embroidered slippers from Hungary. | Romanian rustic woodcarving.

Serbia

Serbian crafts are plentiful and prices are reasonable. Among the most classic buys are embroidery, lace, all kinds of woollens such as sweaters, ponchos, gloves and socks, sometimes quite coarse in texture but incredibly warm. You'll also see sheepskin slippers, as well as ceramics, baskets and woodcarvings of figurines, chess sets, salad servers and so on. Also consider the Turkish legacy: copper coffee pots, filigree jewellery, leather articles — handbags, wallets, belts, jackets and oriental-type slippers.

Try to bargain on the markets. Even in the most serious shops, you may be granted a 10 per cent discount if you pay cash.

Slovakia

For souvenirs look in the shops of the Old Quarter selling embroidery and lace, handpainted porcelain, jewellery, wood carvings and fine crystal glass. The word Starozitnosti indicates an antique shop, but not everything inside will be old; you may find attractive drawings, watercolours and prints as well as bric-a-brac and assorted junk. A characteristic Slovak craft is wire-smithing, creating decorative objects such as birds, animals or farm carts by shaping wire. Many toys are charming, especially the comical carved wooden animals.

Hungarian Porcelain. Ceramics and porcelain are among the most popular products with visitors to Hungary. Two names in particular stand out. The Herend Porcelain Factory is based in the town of Herend near Lake Balaton and has been making exquisite hand-painted vases, dishes, bowls and statuettes since 1826. Herend has proved especially popular with royalty — satisfied customers include Queen Victoria, Kaiser Wilhelm I, the Shah of Iran and Prince Charles. Find out why at the main Herend shop behind Vörösmarty tér on V. József Nádor tér 11.

Zsolnay porcelain from Pécs might not be able to claim as famous a client list, but its products have been far more prominently placed. The company developed a line in brilliant weatherproof ceramic tiles in the late 19th century, and these adorn the rooftops of Matthias Church, the Central Market and the Museum of Applied Arts. Check out their modern Art Nouveau-influenced designs at V. Kígyó utca 4.

Marguerite Martinoli

THE HARD FACTS

To help you plan your trip, here are some of the practical details you need to know about the lands along the Danube.

Climate

Most of the Danube valley has a continental climate. Winters can be harsh, with occasional snow; in January and February the temperature may drop to −15°C (−9°F). In summer it can climb to 30°C (86°F) or more, and the cities in particular can become very hot and humid, especially in July and August. It is cooler and more pleasant in the mountains or on the Black Sea coast. From April to June, September and early October are likely to be pleasantly warm. Showers are possible, even occasional thunderstorms.

Communications

Most mobile phones are compatible with at least one service provider in each country. If you are using the fixed line system, it is cheaper to use public telephones with a telecard rather than hotels. To make international calls, dial the access code, 00, followed by the country code and number, usually omitting the initial 0. The country code to call Austria is 43, Bulgaria 359, Croatia 385, Germany 49, Hungary 36, Romania 40, Serbia 381, Slovakia 421. The code for calling USA and Canada is 1, for UK 44.

Internet cafés are to be found in every town and city, and larger hotels have business centres with internet access. Many big towns have free WiFi areas.

Customs Controls

When crossing borders between EU and non-EU countries, or between two non-EU countries, passengers over 17 can carry, duty-free, up to 200 cigarettes or 50 cigars or 250 g of tobacco, 1 litre of spirits, 1 litre of wine (2 l for some countries), a bottle of perfume. Within the EU, you can carry much larger amounts, but only goods on which duty has been paid.

Emergencies

Most European countries have adopted the common emergency telephone number 112, which also applies to GSM mobile phones.

Help from your consulate is only for critical situations, lost passports or worse, not lost cash or tickets.

Essentials
You will need comfortable walking shoes, a sun hat, sun-block with a high protection factor and insect repellent. It is worth taking an umbrella. Take lightweight cotton clothes in summer, with a sweater or wrap for the cooler evenings. People tend to dress elegantly for the theatre, concerts and the opera.

Etiquette
Old-world courtesies have not been forgotten in central and eastern Europe, where men may still kiss a lady's hand when introduced. If you are invited into someone's home, take a bouquet of flowers and a small gift.

No shorts or miniskirts are allowed for visits of churches or monasteries in Serbia, Bulgaria or Romania. Women are expected to cover their heads, while men should remove their hats.

In Bulgaria, things can be confusing for foreigners at times but can also be fun as nodding the head means "no" and shaking it, "yes".

Formalities
You will need a valid passport. No special health certificates are required by European or North American citizens.

Health
There is a reciprocal health care agreement between EU countries from which you can benefit in case of emergency if you carry a European Health Card. Travellers from outside the EU should ensure that they have adequate medical insurance.

Medical services are of a good standard. Many doctors and dentists speak some English. It is advisable to carry supplies of any medications that you require regularly as the same brands may not be available.

Media
The principal foreign newspapers are sold in kiosks on the day of publication. Hotels usually have satellite TV with the main English-language news channels such as BBC World and CNN.

Money
Currency in **Austria**, **Germany** and **Slovakia** is the Euro, divided into 100 cents.

In **Bulgaria**, the *Lev* (BGL) is divided into 100 *stotinki*. Coins range from 1 to 50 *stotinki* and 1 *lev*, banknotes from 2 to 100 *leva*. The target date for adopting the Euro is 2013, but usually you can already pay in euros in the big tourist shops.

In **Croatia**, the *kuna* (HRK) is divided into 100 *lipa*. Frequently used coins from 1 to 50 *lipa* and 1 to 5 *kuna*, notes from 10 to 200 *kuna*. The Euro is often accepted.

In **Hungary**, the *forint* (Ft. or HUF) is issued in coins from 5 to 200 Ft and banknotes from 500 to 20,000 Ft. Retain all currency exchange receipts to re-exchange *forints* when leaving the country. Do not change money on the street. Hungary is expected to adopt the Euro in 2014 at the earliest.

The currency in **Romania** is the *leu* (plural *lei*), abbreviated RON, divided into 100 *bani*. Frequently used coins range from 5 to 50 *bani*; banknotes from 1 to 100 *lei*. The country is expected to adopt the Euro in 2014.

In **Serbia**, the currency is the *dinar* (CSD). Coins range from 1 to 20 *dinars*, banknotes from 10 to 5000 *dinars*.

Money can be changed at banks and exchange offices, and generally also at railway stations and post offices, automatic cash-distributors are easy to find, usually outside banks. They may charge a handling fee.

The major international credit cards are accepted in hotels, restaurants and large shops. Travellers cheques can be changed in banks and exchange bureaux. US dollars are quite widely accepted, as are euros.

Opening Hours

Banks

Austria. Mon–Fri 8 or 9 a.m.–3 or 3.30 p.m., till 5 p.m. on Thursdays. Small branches may close for lunch from 12.30 to 1.30 p.m.

Bulgaria. Mon–Fri 8.30 a.m.–12.30 p.m. and 1.30–3.30 p.m., Sat 8.30–11.30 a.m.

Croatia. Mon–Fri 7.30 a.m.–7.30 p.m., Sat 7.30 a.m.–noon.

Germany. Mon–Fri 9 or 10 a.m.–12.30 p.m. and 1.30–4 or 5 p.m. (longer hours on Thurs, shorter on Wed or Fri).

Hungary. Mon–Fri 9 a.m.–2 p.m., Sat 9 a.m.–noon.

Romania. Mon–Fri 9 a.m.–noon and 1–3 p.m.

Serbia. Mon–Fri 8 a.m.–7 p.m., Sat 8 a.m.–3 p.m.

Slovakia. Generally open Mon–Fri 8 a.m.–5 p.m.

Post offices

Across the region, post offices generally open Mon–Fri 8 a.m.–6 p.m., and sometimes also Sat 8 or 9 a.m.–noon or 2 p.m. In Austria most close for lunch, from noon to 2 p.m.

Shops

Austria. Generally Mon–Fri 9 a.m.–6 or 6.30 p.m., Sat 9 a.m.–5 p.m. Some have late closing Thurs or Fri to 7.30 p.m.

Bulgaria. Mon–Fri 10 a.m.–8 p.m., Sat 8 a.m.–2 p.m.

Croatia. Mon–Fri 8 a.m.–7 p.m., Sat 8 a.m.–2 p.m.

Germany. Most shops open Mon–Fri 9 or 10 a.m.–7 or 8 p.m.; on Sat shops close earlier.

Hungary. Mon–Fri 10 a.m.– 6 p.m. (Thurs to 8 p.m.), Sat 9 a.m.–1 p.m., food shops open as early as or 7 a.m.

Romania. Mon–Sat 8 a.m.–8 p.m., Sat 8 a.m.–3 p.m. Food shops open longer (6 a.m.–9 p.m.); some even stay open 24 hours a day.

Serbia. Mon–Fri 8 a.m.–noon and 5–8 p.m., Sat 8 a.m.–3 p.m. The larger shops in cities and tourist areas do not close at midday.

Slovakia. Usually open Mon–Fri 9 a.m.–6 or 7 p.m., Sat 9 a.m.–noon or 1 p.m. Some shops also open on Sunday mornings. Smaller shops close for lunch noon–2 p.m.

Photography

Some museums allow you to take photographs but generally without using the flash; check that yours is switched off. Don't even think of taking pictures of military installations.

You will need a spare memory card for your digital camera, and don't forget your battery charger.

Public Holidays

Austria

January 1	New Year's Day
January 6	Epiphany

May 1	Labour Day
August 15	Assumption
October 26	National Day
November 1	All Saints
December 8	Immaculate Conception
December 25	Christmas
December 26	St Stephen's Day

Moveable: Easter Monday, Ascension, Whit Monday, Corpus Christi

Bulgaria

January 1	New Year's Day
March 3	National Day
May 1	Labour Day
May 6	Army Day
May 24	Culture and Education Day (Saints Cyril and Methodius)
September 6	Unification Day
September 22	Independence Day
December 24	Christmas Eve
Dec. 25–26	Christmas

Moveable: Orthodox Good Friday and Easter Monday

Croatia

January 1	New Year's Day
January 6	Epiphany
May 1	Labour Day
June 22	Anti-Fascism Day
June 25	National Day
August 5	Thanksgiving Day
August 15	Assumption
October 8	Independence Day
November 1	All Saints' Day
December 25	Christmas Day
December 26	St Stephen's Day

Moveable: Easter Monday, Corpus Christi

Germany (Bavaria)

Holidays in Germany are determined by each state; these are for Bavaria.

January 1	New Year's Day
January 6	Epiphany
May 1	Labour Day
August 15	Assumption
October 3	Day of Unity
November 1	All Saints
Dec. 25 26	Christmas

Moveable: Good Friday, Easter Monday, Ascension, Whit Monday, Corpus Christi.

Hungary

January 1	New Year's Day
March 15	National Day
May 1	Labour Day
August 20	National Day (St Stephen's)
October 23	Republic Day
November 1	All Saints
Dec. 25–26	Christmas

Moveable: Easter Monday, Whit Monday

Romania

January 1	New Year's Day
January 2	New Year's Holiday
May 1	Labour Day
August 15	Dormition of the Theotokos
December 1	National Day
Dec. 25–26	Christmas

Moveable: Orthodox Easter Monday, Whit Monday

Serbia

January 1	New Year's Day
January 2	New Year's Holiday
January 7	Orthodox Christmas
January 27	St Sava Day*
February 15	Constitution Day
May 1, 2	Labour Days
May 9	Victory Day*
June 28	St Vitus Day*
December 25	Christmas Day**
December 26	St Stephen's Day**

Moveable: Orthodox Good Friday, Orthodox Easter Monday
*working holidays
**observed by Christians

Slovakia

January 1	Foundation Day
January 6	Epiphany
May 1	Labour Day
May 8	Liberation Day
July 5	St Cyril and St Methodius
August 29	Slovak National Uprising
September 1	Constitution Day
September 15	Our Lady of Sorrows
November 1	All Saints Day
November 17	Freedom and Democracy Day
Dec. 24–26	Christmas

Moveable: Good Friday, Easter Monday

Public Transport

The big cities are served by networks of buses, trams and metro systems which are reliable and inexpensive. They mostly operate from 4.30 a.m. to midnight.

Although more expensive in Germany and Austria, taxis are generally good value elsewhere along your route, and a convenient way to get around cities such as Belgrade, Budapest and Bucharest. However, make sure the meter is working, switched on and set to zero before you set off. If there is no meter, agree the price in advance.

Inter-city train services are generally excellent.

Safety

The cities are fairly safe by Western standards. It is nonetheless worth taking some basic precautions. When you go sightseeing, leave your valuables and important documents in your hotel or cruise ship safe. Only carry the money you will need for the day along with a credit card. Watch out for pickpockets in tourist areas and on public transport, and beware of scams (such as money changing and phoney "distractions") aimed at foreigners, which will end up with you and your money parting company.

Sales tax (VAT)

A tax averaging 20 per cent is imposed on most goods in the EU member states, and in most other European countries. To benefit from a tax refund, your purchase in any one store must be above a certain minimum amount: look for the Tax Free for Tourists sign. The sales assistant will give you a Tax Refund Cheque (TRC) and all the necessary information on how to redeem it for cash. When you leave the last EU country on your itinerary, take the TRC with your purchases, receipts and passport to the Customs desk to get it stamped. There may be a Tax Free booth near the Customs desk where your stamped TRC can be redeemed immediately, or you can mail the papers back to the store in the envelope they will have provided. For more information and advice see the site: www.global-blue.com.

Time

Austria, Croatia, Germany, Hungary, Serbia, Slovakia: GMT +1 in winter, GMT +2 from end March to end October.
Bulgaria, Romania: GMT +2 in winter, GMT +3 from end March to end October.

Tipping

Austria. A service charge is included in restaurant bills, but it is customary to round up the bill by about 10%. You should also leave a small tip in cafés. Tips for taxi drivers are about 10 per cent.

Bulgaria. A tip of around 10 per cent is customary for waiters and taxi drivers.

Croatia. Waiters and taxi drivers are tipped around 10–12 per cent.

Germany. A service charge is usually included. A small extra tip is at your discretion. Taxi fares are rounded up by about 10 per cent.

Hungary. Waiters and taxi drivers expect a tip of 10–15 per cent.

Romania. In restaurants the tip is often included; otherwise it is usual to leave around 10 per cent. Taxi drivers hope for a tip from foreigners.

Serbia. A 10 per cent tip is expected in restaurants and by taxi drivers.

Slovakia. A tip of around 10 per cent is usual in restaurants and for taxi drivers.

Waiters often leave a space for an extra tip on credit card vouchers, and leave the total blank. Be sure to fill these in.

Toilets

Public facilities are generally clean, and are usually marked with the usual male and female figures. If there is an attendant, leave a small tip.

Voltage.

220–240V AC, 50 Hz. Plugs are mainly of the two round pin type.

Water

Tap water may taste chlorinated, but a wide choice of sparkling and still mineral water is available in shops and restaurants.

On deck in time to capture the Walhalla
monument as the ship floats past.

LANDMARKS AT A GLANCE

The following table lists the landmarks on the left and right banks of the Danube, shown graphically on the fold-out maps "Landmarks left and right".

Legend:

- 🏰 Castle
- ⛪ Church
- Monastery
- Ruins
- Archaeological site
- Bridge
- Industry
- Power station
- Lock
- Noteworthy building
- Nature
- R Right Bank
- L Left Bank

km	Bank	Symbols	Feature	Region	County
2227		Castle, Church	**Passau**		AT-DE
2203		Lock, Power station	Jochenstein		
2187			Schlögener Loop		
2162		Lock, Power station	Aschach		
2147		Lock, Power station	Ottensheim-Wilhering		
2135		Bridge	**Linz**, Nibelungen Bridge		
2120		Lock, Power station	Abwinden-Asten		
2112	L		Mauthausen		
	R		Confluence with the Enns		
2095		Lock, Power station	Wallsee-Mitterkirchen		
2084		Noteworthy building	Dornach		
2079	L		Grein	A	
	R	Ruins	Freyenstein		AT
2060	R	Lock, Power station	Ybbs-Persenbeug		
	L	Castle	Schloss Persenbeug		
2050	L		Marbach	1	
	L	Church	Maria Taferl pilgrimage church		
2038		Lock, Power station	Melk		
2036	R	Nature	**Melk,** Stift Melk		
2032	R	Castle	Schönbühel Castle		
2025	R	Ruins	Aggstein Castle		
2024	L	Archaeological site	Willendorf	2	
2019	L		Spitz		

A. Strudengau, narrowing of the Danube Valley

1. Nibelungengau
2. Wachau

km		Description	
2019	L	Burg Hinterhaus	
2013	L	Weissenkirchen	
2009	L	**Dürnstein**	2
	L	Prison of Richard the Lion-Heart	
2002	R	Stift Göttweig, 5km south of the river	
	L	**Krems**	
	L	Gozzoburg, several churches	
1980		Altenwörth	3
1977	R	abandoned nuclear power station of Zwentendorf	
1963	R	Tulln	
1949		Greifenstein	
1943	L	DDSG shipyard Korneuburg	AT
1939	R	Klosterneuburg	
1934		**Vienna**	
	R	Danube Canal to Vienna's Innenstadt	
1932	R	Hochhaus Millennium Tower	
1929	L	UNO-City	
1928		Reichsbrücke	
1921		Wien-Freudenau	
1890		Roman settlement of Carnuntum	
1884	R	Hainburg	4
	R	Castle on the Braunsberg	
1880	L	Confluence with the Morava	
	L	Devín Castle	SK-AT
1870	L	Bratislava Castle	
1869	L	**Bratislava**	
1866	L	Branch-off Little Danube/Malý Dunaj	
1853	R	(Lock and) branch-off main arm of Danube and Mosoni Duna	SK
		Danubiana Art Museum	
1821		Gabčíkovo	B
	R	Lock in Gabčíkovo Canal at canal km 10	
1811	L	Confl. Gabčíkovo Canal and main Danube branch	
1768	L	Komárno fortress	
	R	Komárom fortress	HU-SK
1766	L	Confluence with the Váh	
1719	L	Stúrovo	

B. Gabčíkovo Canal, 38.5 km long   3. Tulln Basin

2. Wachau   4. Donau-Auen National Park

km		Description		
1719	🍽	Maria-Valeria Bridge		HU-SK
1718	R	**Esztergom**		
	R ⛪	Esztergom Basilica		
1708	L	Confluence with the Ipoly		
1695	R 🏛	**Visegrád**	5	
	R	Branch-off Szentendre-Danube		
1680	L	**Vác**		
1667	R	**Szentendre**	C	
1663	L ⛪	Church by Imre Makovecs in Göd		
1657	R	Southern tip of Szentendre Island		
1655	R ⋰	Roman city of Aquincum		
1648	R ⛪	**Budapest**, Matthias Church		
	L ❗	Parliament Buildings		
1647	🍽	Chain Bridge		
1580	R ⋰	Roman army base of Intercisa		HU
1578	R 🏭	Dunaújváros industrial city		
1531	R	Paks		
1526	R ❗ ☢	Atomic power station Paks		
1516	L	**Kalocsa,** 5 km from the river		
1499	🍽	Motorway bridge		
1497	R	Confluence with the Sió from Balaton	D	
1480	🍽	Rail and road bridge		
1479	L	Baja, port	6	
1447	R	**Mohács**, port		
1433	R	Hungarian-Croatian frontier		
1425	R 🍽	Batina		
	R	Batina-Bezdan road bridge		
1401	L	Apatin	7	
	L ❗	Jelen brewery		
1383	R	Confluence with Drava		
1366	🍽	Road and rail bridge		CR-RS
1333	R	Vukovar, port		
	R ❗	Water tower		
1299	R	Ilok		
	R ⛪	Franciscan monastery on hilltop		
1298	L	Bačka Palanka	8	

C. Szentendre-Danube
D. Gemenc Nature Reserve
5. Danube Bend

6. Duna-Drava National Park
7. Kopački Rit Nature Reserve
8. Fruška Gora National Park

km	Bank	Icon	Landmark		
1297		🌉	Road bridge		8
1255	L		Novi Sad		
1255	R	❗	Petrovaradin fortress		
1246	R		Sremski Karlovci		
1232		🌉	Motorway bridge		
1214	L		Mouth of the Tisa (Tisza)		
1173	R	🏛	Zemun fortress		RS
1170	R		Mouth of the Sava		
	R		**Belgrade**		
	R	❗	Fortress in Kalemegdan Park		
1167		🌉	Road and rail bridge		
1116	R		Smederevo, port		
	R	❗	Fortress		
1113		🌉	Pipeline bridge		
1112		🌉	Road bridge		
1094	R		Kostolac		
1077	R		Ottoman fortress at Ram		
1075	L		Mouth of the Nera River		
1059	R		Veliko Gradište, port		
1048	L		Moldova Veche, port		
1045		🌉	Disused bridge to Moldova Veche island		
1043	R		Golubac, port		
1041	L	🌳	Babakai rock		
	L	🏛	Laszlo fortress		
1039	R	🏛	Golubac fortress	E	
1018	L		Berzasca		RO-RS
1016	L		Drencova, once the end of the Danube cruise		9
1011	R	⁖	Memorial to Roman emperors, including Tiberius	F	
1004	R	⁖	Stone Age settlement of Lepenski Vir		
999	R	🌳	Greben rock		
991	R		Donji Milanovac, port		
	L	❗	Tri Cule: two watchtowers in the river		
970	L		Dubova	H	
967	L	⛪	Maraconia church	G	
	L	❗	Relief of Decebalus		
965	R	⁖	Tabula Traiana	I	

E. Golubac Klissura and Ljubkova basin
F. Upper Klissura, former cataracts
G. Lower Klissura, former cataracts

H. Upper Kazan, narrows
I. Lower Kazan, narrows
9. Đerdap National Park

km	Bank		Description		
956	R		Tekija		
954	L		Orşova, port		9
	L	⛵	St Anna		
953	L	🏭	Shipyards		
943	⊕	⛴	Đerdap 1	J	RO-RS
934	R		Kladovo, port		
931	L		Drobeta-Turnu Severin, port		
929	L	⁚⁚	Remains of Roman bridge		
863	⊕	⛴	Đerdap 2		
846	R		Mouth of Timok river		
795	L	🏭	Calafat		
790	R		Vidin, port		
	R	‼	Vidin fortress		
743	R		Lom		
700	R		Kozloduj		
	R	‼	Christo Botev Memorial		
636	R		Mouth of the Iskar		
630	L	🏭	Corabia, sugar refinery		
608	R	🏭	Somovit, port		
597	R		Nikopol, port		
	L	🏭	Turnu Magurele, chemical industry	K	RO-BG
554	R		Svištov, southernmost point of the Danube		
537	R		Mouth of the Jantra		
495	R		Ruse, most important Danube port of Bulgaria		
493	L		Giurgiu, port		
489	🏛		Friendship Bridge, for road and rail		
430	L		Olteniţa, port		
	L	🏭	Shipyards, industry		
385	R	🌳	Srebarna Biosphere Reserve		
376	R		Silistra, port		
371	L		Branch-off of Braţul Borcea		
300	🏛		Historic road and rail bridge		L
	R		Cernavodă		RO
	R		Branch-off Danube-Black Sea Canal		
			(Canalul Dunărea-Marea Neagră)		
261	R	⛪	Orthodox church of Ghindăreşti		

J. Iron Gate
K. Belene Island,
   former penitentiary

L. Balta Ialomiţei
9. Đerdap National Park

km	Bank		Landmark		
253	R		Hârşova	L	
248	L		Confluence with Braţul Borcea		RO
239	L		Giurgeni		
		🚉	Road bridge		
236	R		Branch-off Braţul Măcin		
170	L		Brăila	M	
	R		Confluence with Braţul Măcin		
155	L		Mouth of Siretul (Siret/Sereth)		
150	L		Galaţi,		
	L		biggest Danube port for sailing ships		
134	L		Mouth of the Prut		RO-MD
133	L		Border between Moldova and Ukraine		
128	L		Reni, petrol port		
103	R		Isaccea		RO-UA
80	L		Branch-off Braţul Chilia		
			= border between Romania and Ukraine		
71	R		Tulcea		10
63	R		Branch-off Braţul Sfântu Gheorghe		RO
0	R		Sulina		
	L	❗	Lighthouse		

L. Balta Ialomiţei   10. Danube Delta National Park
M. Balta Brăilei

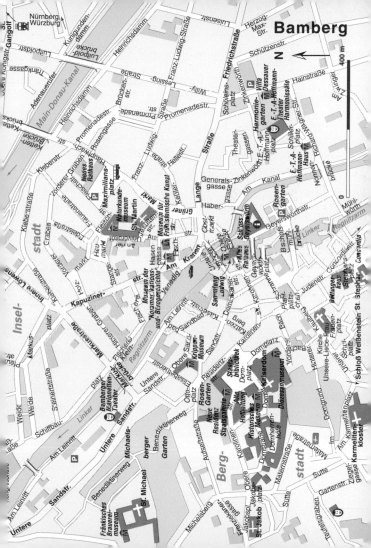

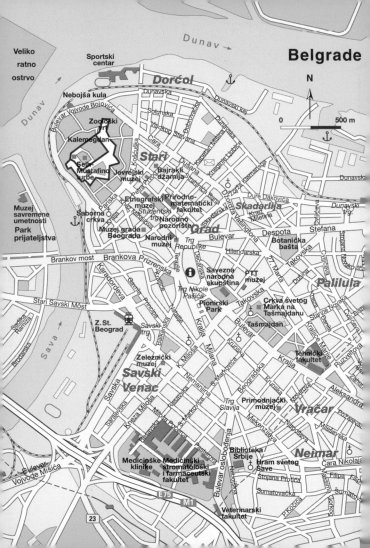

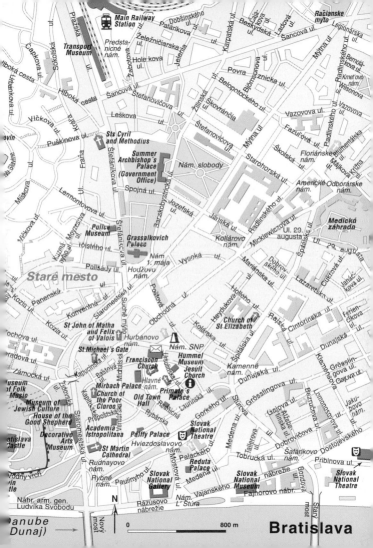

Central Budapest

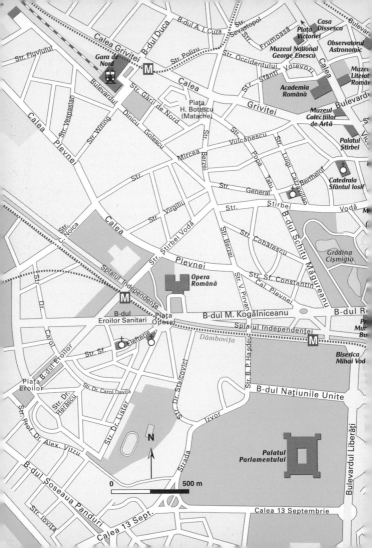

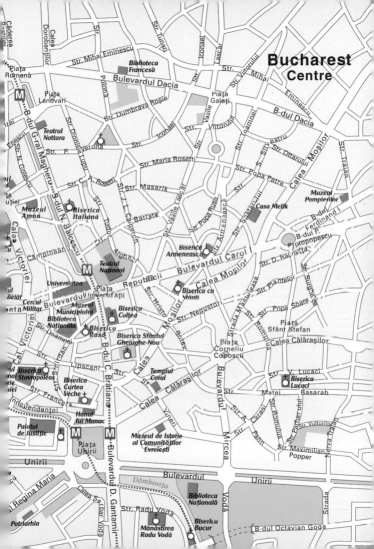

Bucharest Centre

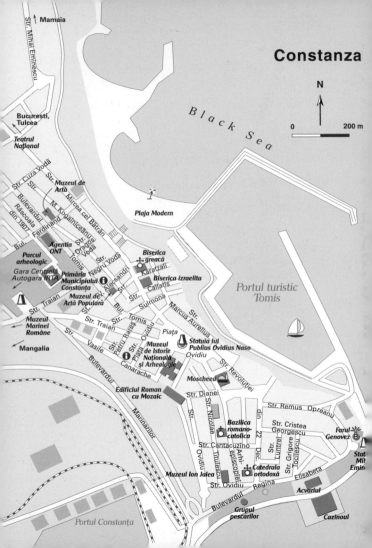

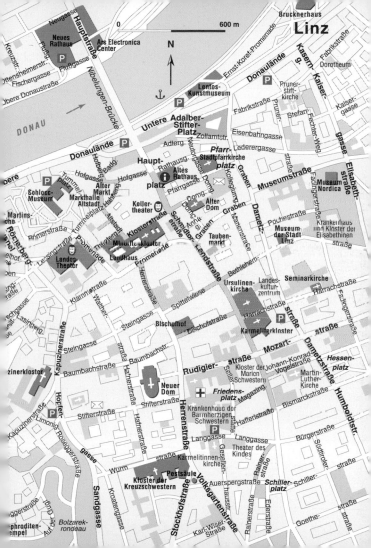

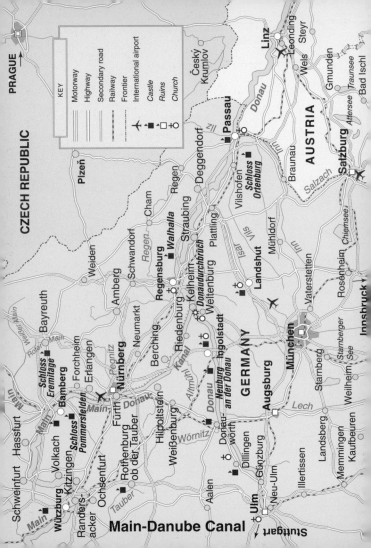

Main-Danube Canal

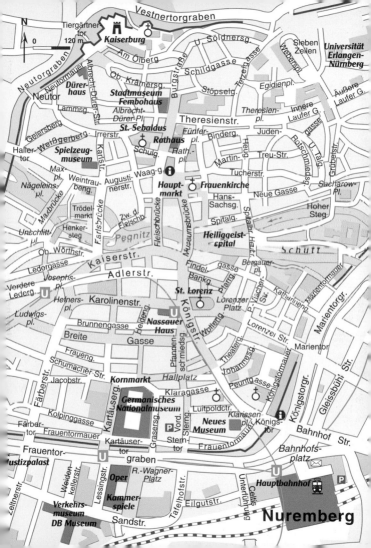

Nuremberg

Map labels (reading across the map):

N

0   120 m

Vestnertorgraben

Tiergärtner tor

Kaiserburg

U Söldnerg.

Sieben Zellen

Universität Erlangen-Nürnberg

Am Ölberg

Schildgasse

Wenzelsp.

Neutorgraben

Ob. Krämersg.

Burgstraße

Terzelgasse

Egidienpl.

Äußere Laufer G.

Albrecht-Dürer-Str.

Dürer-haus

Stadtmuseum Fembohaus

Stöpselg.

Theresien-pl.

Innere Laufer G.

Neutormauer

Weißgerberg.

Neutor

Lammsg.

Albrecht-Dürer-Pl.

Theresienstr.

Juden-

Rotschmiedsg.

U. Talg.

Gelersberg

St. Sebaldus

Rathaus

Fünfer-pl.

Binderg.

Heug.

Treu-Str.

Grübelstr.

Haller-tor

Irrerstr.

Schulg.

Rath.-pl.

Martin-

Sacharow-Pl.

Spielzeug-museum

Karlstr.

Augusti-nerstr.

Waag-g.

Hauptmarkt

Frauenkirche

Tucherstr.

Neue Gasse

Max-pl.

Weintrau-beng.

Hans-Sachsg.

Spitalg.

Hoher Steg

Nägeleins-pl.

Madbrücke

Trödel-markt

Zw. d. Fleischb.

Fleischbrücke

Museumsbrücke

Spitalbr.

Halte-

Schutt

Unschlitt-pl.

Henker-steg

Karlsbrücke

Pegnitz

Heiliggeist-spital

Ob. Wörthstr.

Kaiserstr.

Findel-

gasse

Bergauer-pl.

Ledergasse

Adlerstr.

Bank-g.

Pfarrg.

Lacher-

Marientormauer

Vordere Lederg.

Josephs-pl.

St. Lorenz

Lorenzer Platz

Str.

Katharineng.

Heiners-pl.

Karolinenstr.

Königstr.

Lorenzer Str.

Marientorgr.

Ludwigs-pl.

Brunnengasse

Heideng.

Wölfel-

Marientor

Breite

Gasse

Nassauer Haus

Theaterg.

Johannesg.

Königstormauer

Fraueng.

Pfannen-schmiedsg.

Peuntgasse

Gleisbühl-Str.

Schumacher-Str.

Hallplatz

Kornmarkt

Klaragasse

Marientor

Färberstr.

Jacobstr.

Germanisches Nationalmuseum

Luitpoldstr.

Neues Museum

Klarissen-pl.

Königstorgr.

Bahnhof Str.

Kolpinggasse

Kartäuserg.

P

Vord.

Sterng.

Klarissen-pl.

Königs-tor

Färber-tor

Frauentormauer

Kartäuser-tor

Graserg.

Stern-tor

Frauentormauer

Bahnhofs-platz

Frauentor-

Justizpalast

graben

R.-Wagner-Platz

Tafelhofstr.

Celtis Unterführung

Hauptbahnhof

Weiden-kellerstr.

Oper

Lessingstr.

P

Zeltnerstr.

Verkehrs-museum DB Museum

Kammer-spiele

Sandstr.

Eilgutstr.

Nuremberg

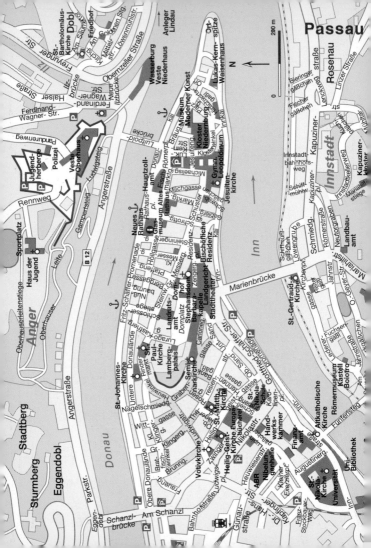

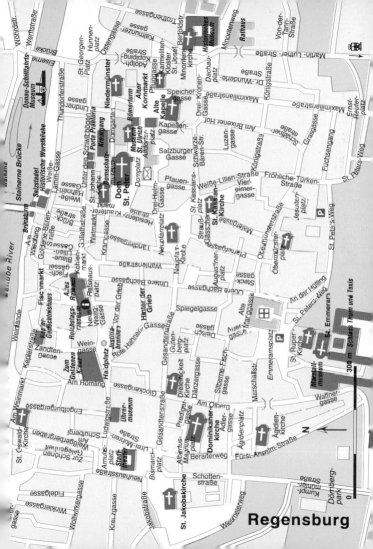

Regensburg

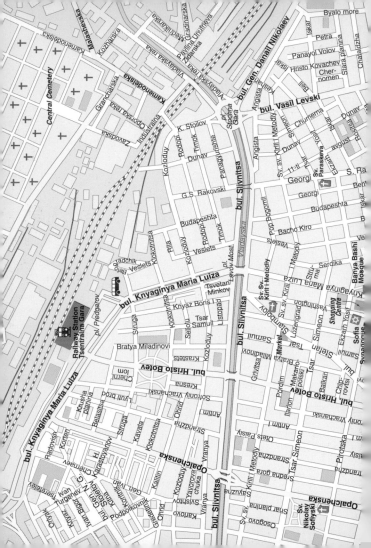

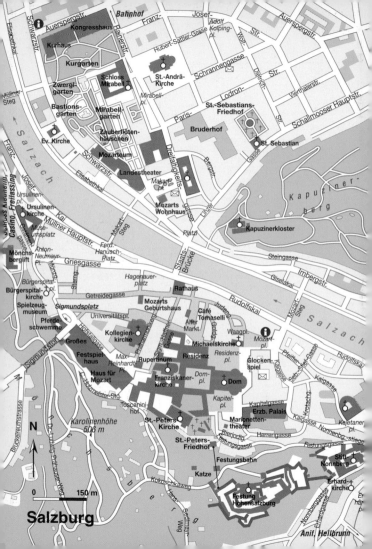

Salzburg

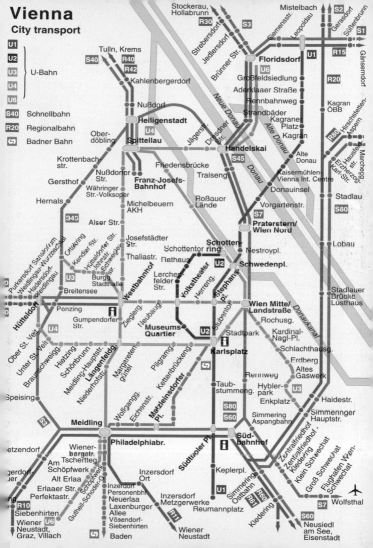

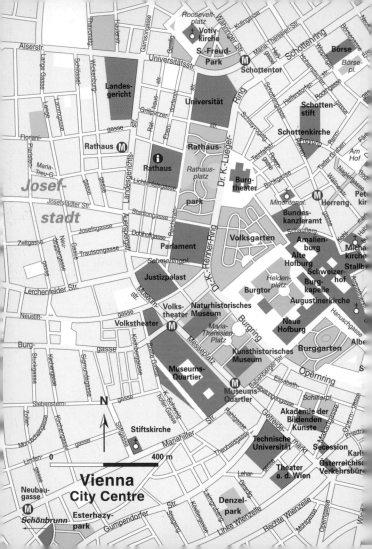

Vienna
City Centre

Josef-
stadt

N

0   400 m

Roosevelt-platz
Votiv-kirche
S.-Freud-Park
Schottentor
M
Börse
Börse-pl.

Universitätsstr.
Universität
Landes-gericht
Rathaus
M
Rathaus
Rathaus-platz
park
Rathaus-platz
Burg-theater

Schotten-stift
Schottenkirche
Am Hof
Bundes-kanzleramt
Herreng.
M
Pet-kir

Parlament
Volksgarten
Amalien-burg
Alte Hofburg
Schweizer-hof
Micha-kirche
Stallb

Justizpalast
Helden-platz
Burg-kapelle
Augustinerkirche

Volks-theater
Naturhistorisches Museum
Burgtor
Neue Hofburg
Burggarten
Albe

M
Volkstheater
Maria-Theresien-Platz
Kunsthistorisches Museum
Opernring

Museums-Quartier
M
Museums-Quartier
Schillerpl.
Akademie der Bildenden Künste
Secession
Karls
Österreichische Verkehrsbür

Stiftskirche
Technische Universität
Theater a. d. Wien

Neubau-gasse
M
Schönbrunn
Esterhazy-park
Denzel-park

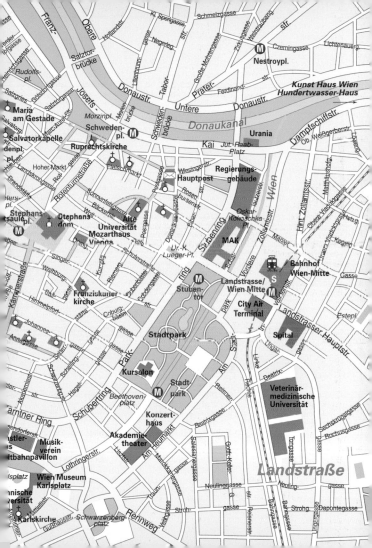

General editor
Barbara Ender-Jones

Translation, editorial assistance
Jack Altman

Research, technical assistance
Elke Frey

Design
Karin Palazzolo

Layout
Karin Palazzolo
Matias Jolliet

Photo credits
p. 1 Romanian Tourist Office (Iron Gate); p. 2 Corbis.com

Maps
JPM Publications,
Mathieu Germay
Jonathan Reymond

Copyright © 2011, 2008
JPM Publications S.A.
12, avenue William-Fraisse,
1006 Lausanne, Switzerland
information@jpmguides.com
http://www.jpmguides.com/

Every care has been taken to verify the information in the guide, but the publisher cannot accept responsibility for any errors that may have occurred. If you spot an inaccuracy or a serious omission, please let us know.

Printed in Germany
12183.00.9178
Edition 2011